B6

Aqu
1992

Aquarius 1992

Teri King's complete horoscope
for all those whose birthdays fall between
21 January and 19 February

Pan Astral
London, Sydney and Auckland

First published 1991 by Pan Books Ltd,
Cavaye Place, London SW10 9PG
© Teri King 1991
ISBN 0 330 30950 1

Phototypeset by Input Typesetting, London
Printed in England by Clays Ltd, St Ives plc

Contents

Introduction

Astrology is a very complex science. While it can be useful in assessing the different aspects of human relationships, there are many misconceptions associated with it. Not the least of these is the cynic's question: 'How can zodiac forecasts be accurate for all the millions of people born under any one sign?' The answer is that all horoscopes published in newspapers, books and magazines are, of necessity, of a general nature. Unless an astrologer can work from the date, time and place of your birth, the reading given will only be true for the typical member of your sign.

Take a person born on 1 May. This person is principally a subject of Taurus, simply because the Sun occupies that portion of the heavens known as Taurus during the period 21 April to 21 May. However, there are other influences to be taken into account, for instance the Moon: this planet enters a fresh sign every forty-eight hours. On the birth date in question it may have been in, say, Virgo – and if that were the case it would make this particular subject a Taurean/Virgoan. Then again the rising sign or Ascendant must also be taken into consideration. This also changes constantly, as approximately every two hours a new sign passes over the horizon. The rising sign is of utmost importance, determining the image projected by the subject to the outside world – in effect, the personality. (This is why the time of birth is essential for compiling a natal chart.) Let us suppose that in this particular instance Taurus was rising at the time of birth; this would make the individual a Taurean/Virgoan/Taurean. Now, because two of the three main influences are Taurus, the subject would be a fairly typical Taurean, displaying the faults and attributes associated with this sign. But if the Moon and the Ascendant were, say, in Aquarius, the subject would exhibit more of the vices and virtues of a true Aquarian.

For each of the nine planets this procedure is carried on, each making up a significant part of the subject's character; their positions, the signs they occupy, and the aspects formed from one to another all play a part of the make-up. The calculation and interpretation of these movements, the work of the astrologer, will produce an individual's birth chart. Because the heavens are constantly changing, people with identical birth charts are a very rare occurrence, although it could happen with people born at the same time and in the same place. In such a case the deciding factors as to how those individuals differ in their lives, loves, careers, financial prospects and so on would be due to environmental and parental influences.

Returning to the hypothetical Taurean: as has been said he would believe himself typical of the sign; but were the Moon and the Ascendant in the alternative positions stated he would be an Aquarian. So he would get a more dependable reading from the general Aquarian predictions than from the Taurean ones. This explains why some people swear by their newspaper horoscopes, while others can never believe them. But whatever his Moon sign and Ascendant, the Taurean will always display certain characteristics of his birth sign, because of the Sun's influence.

Belief in astrology does not necessarily mean believing we lead totally determined lives, that we are 'fated', or that we have no control over our destiny. What it shows is that our lives run in cycles, for good and for bad; knowing this, with the help of astrology we can make the most of, or minimize, certain patterns and tendencies. How this is done is entirely up to the individual.

For instance, if you know beforehand that you have a lucky period ahead, you can make the most of it by pushing ahead with plans and aspirations – anything that is dear to you. It follows that you can also take more care in times of illness, misfortune, romantic upset and everyday adversity.

Astrology should be used as it was originally intended – as a guide, especially to character. Throughout the ages there has never been found a better guide to character analysis, enabling people to learn and use advantageously the information relating to personality, friendships, work and romance.

Once this invaluable information has been understood it makes it easier for us to see ourselves as we really are and, what's more, as others see us. We can accept our own weaknesses and limitations and those of others. We can evolve from there to inner peace and outer confidence.

In the following pages you will find character, happiness and partnership guides; romantic, health and marriage prospects; punters' luck; monthly and daily forecasts; and an indication of the Moon's influence on your moods. Used wisely, astrology can help you through life. It is not intended to encourage complacency, since in the final analysis it is all up to you. Allow astrology to walk hand in hand with you and success and happiness are virtually guaranteed.

Teri King

A New Look at Your Sun Sign

Most members of the general public appreciate that of necessity Sun sign astrology is fairly general, and that should an individual wish for a more in-depth study then it is essential to hire an astrologer who will proceed to study his client's date, year, place and time of birth. The birth chart is then correlated from the facts.

However, there is a middle way which can be most illuminating. Each Sun sign comprises 30° (or days), and by reducing these down into three sections it is possible to acquire a clearer picture of your sign which is more intimate than the usual method. Therefore, check out your date of birth and draw your own conclusions:

Aquarius (21 January to 19 February)

If you were born between 21 January and 30 January, your Sun falls in the Uranus section of Aquarius. You are a very versatile human being with a restless mind and a nervous, highly-strung nature. Although this section of your sign implies both genius and notoriety, there is nevertheless a tendency towards rebellion inherent in the personality which can make you feel at odds with the strictures within which you live. More aggressive individuals display subversive behaviour in terms of rioting, social uprisings and armed attempts at the destruction of the status quo. Change, innovation and progress are key words to the ideals that this section represents. Often you are so far-sighted that you see beyond your time into future conditions which should be either improved or obliterated. Your personality is friendly, curious, freedom-loving, enthusiastic, personal and very independent. You are fascinated by many things but committed to few. That is probably because your mind is so quick and creative – a plethora of projects can easily overtake you before you have the time to complete any of them. You are a 'people person' who enjoys crowds, parties and social gatherings and meeting new faces. But although you love people you need your own space, and when the situation gets too confining you find a way to remove yourself – mentally if not physically. Romantic happy endings hardly overwhelm you, yet you are likely to feel melancholia watching the evening news. Whatever way you look at

11

it, you are a law unto yourself. People may not always understand this, and sometimes they may not like it, but the chances are that they will respect it. You ask nothing from the world except honesty and justice.

For those who were born between 31 January and 9 February, your Sun falls in the Mercury section of Aquarius. Therefore you are all mind and very little emotion. Your greatest interests and aptitudes are of a scientific and mathematical nature: computing, engineering, medicine, marine biology and scientific research are vocational areas that appeal. Open, honest, gregarious and highly talkative, because your mind is rapid and restless you often have a hard time coordinating your words and thoughts. Probably the idea of some form of writing highly appealed for a long period of your life. However, you first have to develop the discipline to deal with the tedium of the experience, or you will never complete any projects. Your mind is definitely beyond its time. Sometimes you may suffer for this, because people are not willing to accept your new ideas, strictures and forms. However, with persistence your genius will be able to crumble resistance. Your personality is kind, sincere and considerate. Optimism, self-confidence and tenacity – these are all characteristics. Deep within your mind there is a belief in man as a limitless being, and your actions are an extension of this attitude. Defeat never gets you down, because you know how to use it to create a far more substantial success. You are not afraid to use your power; never forget that it's there.

If you were born between 10 February and 19 February, your Sun falls in the Venus section of your sign. You are romantic and tend to get persistently involved with the wrong people. The distance factor is a force which seems to affect your relationships to a considerable degree; this takes the form of falling in love with someone who is married, who lives in another country, whose emotional problems prevent involvement in mature relationships, or who simply does not reciprocate your attraction to them. Romantically, you seek excitement rather than substance and have a restless nature which swiftly spurs you on. You are pleasure-loving, impulsive, changeable and fickle. In your youthful years you see love as an exciting kind of game whose components are ever-changing. However, you are generous and idealistic and more sensitive than other Aquarians. Your personality is charming and yet mysterious. People are sometimes wary of getting close to you because of the contradictory elements in your make-up. It is often difficult to understand what you really feel, because you change your mind so often. Fundamentally, you are a person who is very easy to know but difficult to understand. If someone should abruptly ask you what you want most, you would probably respond with fifteen answers off the top of your head – and then say that you take it all back because you really want none of them . . . then explain that you thought you did! At this point your questioner is totally confused. But that's all right, because as a matter of fact, you are too.

What Makes Aquarians Happy?

Political meetings, demonstrations against any kind of tyranny, good companionship and the truth no matter how much it may hurt – all these bring happiness to Aquarians. They also love to celebrate their birthday a month early and to travel, especially if this is in order to discover what can be done to help their fellow man. They adore their friends and put up with their unpunctuality and eccentricity; are happy to do things spontaneously – such as taking a holiday at the last moment – and love to wear comfortable but not necessarily fashionable clothes. Happiness lies in totally disregarding convention and wearing jeans at a formal function, splashing in puddles and playing snowballs when they are supposed to be long past the age to know better. Being as outrageous as possible is their idea of fun, so the faint-hearted should give them a wide berth.

What Makes Aquarians Unhappy?

They are miserable when they desperately want to go somewhere or be in some particular company, but find it is necessary to 'doll up'; also when they know they *must* be on time for something important. Further unhappiness is caused by man's inhumanity to man – bullies in any guise. Clinging lovers and those who demand an account of exactly how they have spent their time cause further unhappiness, and they are embarrassed if people are over-grateful when they consider they have done the only decent thing possible. They despise the regularity of breakfast at eight, lunch at one and dinner at eight; what happened to genuine hunger, they will enquire, and who needs all that food? Another pet hate is sexual routine, which is a complete turn-off for them. Mother's, Father's and Christmas Days are considered commercialized, over-sentimentalized and their idea of sheer hell. The list of dislikes for this sign is endless, but one must bear in mind that at least they are always sincere in their beliefs and no one can take that away. It is just a question of whether or not people can put up with them!

Partnerships

Aquarius Woman

With Aries Man   (21 March to 20 April)

This woman, constantly surrounded by others in active debate, will attract Aries who likes activity of any description. Later he will find that her interest in others does not extend to him, and he is basically a self-centred person. This 'me first' attitude will be the basis for many arguments and, if she attacks his sensitive ego, all the force of his fiery temper will be directed at her. The Aquarian likes all relationships to be based on friendship but this is impossible for the Aries to accept, for he finds it impossible to make friends with those other than his own sex. Being a born leader he will resent the fact that she has every intention of following a career of her own. This will be further aggravated by the Arien possessive streak, which makes him very reluctant to allow her to be involved in any task that does not involve him directly.

With Taurus Man   (21 April to 21 May)

Taurus is a character who enjoys home life, a secure job and the respect of friends and acquaintances. To Aquarius these things are not important; she believes that her energies should be devoted to the good of mankind, not just the well being of one person. She will, for the most part, always be out and about getting involved in all kinds of causes and demonstrations. Here Taurus' jealousy will rear its ugly head, for he knows that whilst she is out, she is quite likely to meet a man who shares this interest. No doubt she will tell him at some point that his attitudes are wrong and that his priorities are somewhat mixed up. Not a well aspected partnership.

With Gemini Man   (22 May to 21 June)

There is a love of communication in this relationship and it will not be long before the two are totally involved in each other. If they do become absorbed in each other's interests a lot of fun will be had. Gemini is the original Jack of all Trades and this will make finding a job rather difficult. The Aquarian also has weaknesses in this direction and this could, of course, lead to financial problems. A switching of roles could take place, each alternatively becoming the bread-winner. She will have to decide, in the end, how the finances are to be handled and, providing she accepts this role, then the relationship could be very happy and stimulating for both parties.

With Cancer Man   (22 June to 22 July)
The Cancerian will appreciate this woman's air of efficiency and involvement, but it will not be until later that he discovers these attributes do not spill over into the domestic routine. He sets great store on his home environment, but she doesn't. Whisking through the housework at breakneck speed, doing only the barest necessities, will not meet with his approval. He feels that she should spend more time in the home rather than out with friends, doing them favours and joining in their meetings. He will even suggest that if she wants to change the world then she should start at home. She will not be amused by this suggestion. This is an unwise partnership, and one in which he is likely to get hurt, quite deeply.

With Leo Man   (23 July to 23 August)
This man has a knack of making people feel important, and this is the characteristic that will make him attractive to Miss Aquarius. Also, her absorption in life will equally attract him. However, his fiery pride and his love of the material things in life will give her much cause for complaint. Leo, being a passionate animal, will derive a lot of hurt and anguish from this detached woman, and his pride will make it almost impossible for him to get to the roots of her apparent coolness. If she fails to respond to his warmth and affection, he will turn to using arrogance and overbearance. She will have to cultivate an interest in the financial side of life, for Leo likes the best things in life even when he cannot afford them, so it would be wise for her to operate the purse strings. A very stormy partnership.

With Virgo Man   (24 August to 23 September)
Their love of communication could be the thing that brings these two together in the first place; she loves a man with a quick intelligent mind such as Virgo's. She is a reformer – trying to change the world into what she believes it should be. However, whilst she is doing this, he will be trying to reform her. When she realizes this she will not be too happy about it. The biggest area of friction will be his critical eye, turned on her at every available opportunity. His insistence that she take on the role of housekeeper will unsettle and irritate her, for she will insist

that household chores be shared, and besides this she has her own career to worry about. Her refusal to come to terms with his budgeting will also be an area for argument. A good friendship, but these two should never become lovers.

With Libra Man   (24 September to 23 October)
Libra's charm and apparent search for harmony will go to make an attractive package for the Aquarian. Her independence and her need for other people will lead him to try and make her a part of his life. She will want to remain independent and take part in the world around her. This won't bother him as long as she can remain feminine and well dressed. He will expect the relationship to remain on a romantic level and will do much to keep it this way. She will be happy with this arrangement as long as she can mildly flirt on occasions. Both are resilient types and should mix well with each other's friends. However, he could instigate worries over finance. On the whole, though, this is a good relationship.

With Scorpio Man   (24 October to 22 November)
The Aquarian woman, whilst famous for her adaptability, will find this relationship extremely hard going. His fixed opinions and intense emotions will not find favour with this humanitarian, especially where outside relationships are concerned. Jealousy is a major part of the Scorpio make-up; he believes it to be a necessary part of love. She, on the other hand, believes that it only serves to kill emotion. Therefore, her social life will cause him to feel resentment. She will never realize that self-expression is impossible for him, and that his over-bearing attitude is only a need for reassurance. There also will be friction where finances are concerned, and her indifference taking care with money will lead to many a scene. Also, her career will come in for some criticism, for he believes that she should be there at all times for his own exclusive use. These two will only serve to destroy each other.

With Sagittarius Man   (23 November to 21 December)
Sagittarius will sense that love, in this woman's life, does not necessarily mean possession, therefore he will be attracted to her. She could easily be attracted to his love of challenge and adventure. This is a relationship in which each will be able to retain their individuality, and will be able to go their own way most of the time. The Sagittarian's emotions, which in general

are short-lived, go very deep, but her detached manner will sometimes stimulate him to find a warmer hearted person. There could also be chaos on the financial front. This will stem from the Sagittarian's tendency to gamble away the funds, and the Aquarian's lack of concern for the material things in life. The good news is that he will encourage and boost her career whenever possible for he does not believe that the man should be the only one in a relationship with a career. A fair relationship, but one that swings from extreme to extreme.

With Capricorn Man   (22 December to 20 January)
It is quite likely that a drifting Miss Aquarius will find herself rescued by this character. His responsible attitude to life will attract her and she will arouse his protective instincts. However, she will soon have to accept the fact that his career comes first, and the more interest she can show in it the better it will be for her. Whenever he sinks into a depression she will have to be there with encouragement. It is no use her being impatient with this pessimism, for that would only lead to violent quarrels. If harmony is to be achieved she will have to put her career second to his. He will object strongly when he finds that she has friends around at all hours, for he is not the sociable type. His tendency to save for the future will be encouraged by this woman who has no need for material things, but she could accuse him of being miserly. This is not a very satisfactory relationship.

With Aquarius Man   (21 January to 19 February)
Intellectual compatability may be the reason for the initial attraction in this case. Because other people believe that their cool façades mean they lack warmth, they will get satisfaction from each other by being able to drop this image together. The nurturing of this relationship should keep them both satisfied, as they both like to see human relationships develop. Life will be challenging for they will be constantly trying to keep up with each other, as she can change her moods and her mind as quickly as he. The financial aspect of the relationship could undermine compatibility, as neither will want to give this subject a lot of thought. However, someone will have to take charge of the purse strings. She will be able to follow her career, for he does not suffer feelings of inferiority, and he will support her in any way he can. This is a good union.

With Pisces Man (20 February to 20 March)
The Piscean's feelings often show when he becomes involved with the affairs of other people, but not so the Aquarian's; she can help out in a detached manner devoid of all emotion. However, the Piscean will not realize this until he has known her for some time. He will believe that there is a true caring soul. In certain moods this man will adore being mothered by her, as she will sometimes adore mothering him. However, it may not always be so easy to get these moods to coincide. If he is desperate for warmth and she is not in the mood to give it, he could accuse her of being cold and heartless. This independent woman will be unable to comply with the wishes of the Piscean who likes to be the centre of his woman's world. She needs to develop her individuality and cannot fulfil this need if she has to think only of him. Money is an aspect of life both characters would prefer to ignore. However, the Aquarian usually possesses more common sense and it will fall to her to take care of the purse strings. This will be a difficult relationship.

Aquarius Man

With Aries Woman (21 March to 20 April)
Miss Aries could find herself on the receiving end of this type's need to change everything. The Aquarian is a reformer; the type who will feel a need to change practically all he comes into contact with, be it his home, his office, his friends – the entire world. However, whilst all this change is going on it is rare that the Aquarian ever really improves anything. He knows what needs to be done, but cannot always find the necessary help to carry things through. Miss Aries will have to be a friend to this man as well as a lover. She also prefers the more sophisticated individuals peopling her world and will find it hard to come to terms with the eccentric types introduced to her by the Aquarian. The Aquarian is also known for his detached attitude to the people in his life, even to those whom he loves. She may be hurt when he is in one of these moods.

With Taurus Woman (21 April to 21 May)
Aquarius is unconventional. He loathes any kind of formality and will not recognize any superiors until they have earned their superiority in his eyes. The material things in life hold no attraction for him, unlike Miss Taurus who needs security. His

intellect is all important and his work will only be enjoyable when it is of an intellectually taxing nature. His emotions are rather on the cool side, hers a lot warmer. He will take no notice of her occasional emotional outbursts. He also dislikes a routine existence, preferring to live from day to day, always helping friends, but in a detached manner. She will resent the amount of time he spends helping others, for she considers that the time should be spent with her. This relationship is nothing short of disastrous and should be avoided wherever possible.

With Gemini Woman   (22 May to 21 June)
This is a relationship that will have at its base the need for intellectual rapport. The physical side of love will hardly enter into things. They will agree on the necessity, as they see it, for a constantly changing circle of friends and interests. However, his constant need to help others in distress, whilst ignoring her needs, could lead to irritation and a little friction. His outside interests will always interfere with the domestic side of life. This situation will lead to a lot of argument for he will not be able to understand her neurosis over what he sees as a trivial matter. He will always be totally honest with her as their relationship deepens, and he will show an interest in everything she does. This is a good union although it is based only on intellectual stimulation.

With Cancer Woman   (22 June to 22 July)
Initially her domestic qualities and her sensitive nature could appeal to the Aquarian, but it won't be long before he wants to change her as he does everything else in this world. Her stubborn character is unlikely to approve of this. Whilst she is proud of her female intuition he is just as proud of his logical outlook, so friction is likely to result. She could provide a good home life for him, but it is hardly likely that he will be there to enjoy it for any length of time. He is always out helping someone or trying to change the world in general. This relationship doesn't have a lot going for it and is therefore unlikely to last for any length of time.

With Leo Woman   (23 July to 23 August)
Miss Leo must accept from the start that she will never find a warmer side to the Aquarian than the one he first shows her. There is no point in her thinking that she will ever uncover some deeper, less detached human being. Fixed opinions and

pride are shared by these two and here could be a reason for friction. He is a born humanitarian, putting the good of mankind before any financial gain; she is totally the other way inclined. She also feels that his ideas are totally unrealistic. She will begin to realize that to this man she must be a friend first and a lover second. She will always have to share in the new interests which constantly appeal to his imagination. Unless both have a lot of determination, this union is unlikely to succeed.

With Virgo Woman   (24 August to 23 September)
Aquarius's involvement with life, and the activity that surrounds him, could be the initial attraction for her. Her efficient and independent manner will lead him to thinking that at last he has found someone who will not lean on him for support. It won't be long though before their basic differences begin to show up. The first will be the fact that, although they both need mental stimulation, his will come from outside sources, whilst she needs hers to come from within the relationship. A quiet evening together could be spoilt by his tendency to bring home friends and their problems. When she realizes this is the pattern of things to come, she will be slightly put out, and will resort to nagging. It is unlikely that these two will have an easy relationship. She should learn to be more adaptable, and he to be a little less opinionated and fixed. This relationship should really be a short affair with no permanent union in view.

With Libra Woman   (24 September to 23 October)
The social whirl, which both love, could well throw these two together. They are both attracted to activity and excitement and unusual people. She will understand when the phone rings in the early hours and he has to rush off to help a friend in need. She might even go with him. However, there are certain areas where they do not agree, but it will be possible for them to reach a compromise over some of these. Their biggest problem could be her sentimental side clashing with the Aquarian sense of logic. This will lead to argument and bruised feelings on her part. However, this should be a stimulating and successful relationship.

With Scorpio Woman   (24 October to 22 November)
The intense emotions of the Scorpion will arouse a dislike in the Aquarian male; he has a strong abhorrence of drama or trauma in any shape or form. As her emotions are such a strong

part of her life she could soon find out that life with the Aquarian, who seems devoid of emotion, is inadequate. Her frequent outbursts will leave him wondering whether or not this lady is unbalanced. She has such a strong jealous streak that she may regard his continuous involvement with the outside world as a threat. However, tension can be eased when she realizes that he regards her as much a friend as a sex object. This is the basis on which a stronger relationship can be built. She will have to contain her strong likes and dislikes, for he too has strong and fixed opinions. He values people and not objects or money, therefore there could be some conflict in this area as he will not be able to understand her worrying over financial matters. This relationship is best avoided.

With Sagittarius Woman   (23 November to 21 December)
Her carefree attitude could easily attract this man as it is like his own. He doesn't like the weaker, clinging types, for they tend to cramp his style. They both believe in living life to the full, he with his humanitarian outlook, she for the social life. However, when the occasion arises where she needs her man, likely as not he will be out administering to some poor unfortunate. This will not go down too well with her and she will feel neglected and, possibly, unloved. It will not be hard for her to meet someone new outside the relationship, and this could be the beginning of an affair. Neither find it easy to concentrate on financial matters, but he is better equipped for this task and it is he who should make the effort in this direction. However, all in all it will be an emotionally uncomfortable union.

With Capricorn Woman   (22 December to 20 January)
Should Miss Capricorn be going through any kind of bad experience she can count on Aquarius to help her out in the emergency. This is when he is at his best. However, her depressions, which he first took on as a challenge, will eventually prove to be too much, even for him, and when he finds his sympathy and optimism are wasted he will take these qualities to a more appreciative person. She will never be able to understand his need to help outsiders, for she thinks that her problems come before all others. But he needs the social and humanitarian involvement. His career will also bring forth an area of friction, for he is likely to get through quite a number of jobs, never really settling in any one for long. She needs security and this sort of behaviour will not give her that. Her need for financial

security is something he will never be able to comprehend; the material side of life leaves him cold. This, as you can see, will not be a satisfactory relationship.

With Aquarius Woman   (21 January to 19 February)
Intellectual compatibility may be the reason for the initial attraction between these two. Because other people believe that their cool façades mean they lack warmth, they will get satisfaction from each other by being able to drop this image together. The nurturing of this relationship should keep them both satisfied, as they both like to see human relationships develop. Life will be challenging for they will constantly be trying to keep up with each other, as she can change her moods and mind as quickly as he. The financial aspect of the relationship could undermine compatibility, as neither will want to give this subject a lot of thought. However, someone will have to take charge of the purse strings. She will be able to follow her career, for he does not suffer feelings of inferiority, and he will support her in any way he can. This is a good union.

With Pisces Woman   (20 February to 20 March)
The Aquarian is constantly involved in the troubles and causes of this world, but it will hardly enter his head to channel some of this concern into his own relationships. Miss Pisces will become bitter if this state of affairs should continue for very long. His detached façade will cause untold damage to her intense emotions, and she will eventually realize that he does not love her as deeply as she thought. However, if she is determined to stay with this man, she should try to channel some of her energy into an artistic hobby of some description, for he will never be able to satisfy this part of her personality. He will, however, encourage her in any activity or career she decides to follow. Her complete lack of responsibility where financial matters are concerned will lead him to take up the purse strings. Anything more than a short, wild affair would be disastrous.

Striking It Rich with the Stars

No matter how talented we may be, without the assistance of Lady Luck most of us would not get very far. We have all heard others say, 'Oh, he was born under a lucky star' or 'She's always falling on her feet'. Whether this is the case or not often depends on our birth sign.

Many of us make our own luck; some are positively followed around by it, while others always seem to be in the wrong place at the wrong time.

We all have a key to good fortune, but most of us never learn how to use it. Read on in order to discover just where you may be going wrong.

*

You possess ideas which are streets ahead of other mere mortals; when you hit the big time it is usually through the sciences or possibly some kind of invention. Your home is full of little gadgets that you thought up when you had nothing better to do than head for the Patent Office next day.

However, it's quite likely that an idealist such as yourself may settle for richness of spirit. You are concerned for the human race, an admirable wish but one which can lead to notoriety rather than riches, though it is quite possible that this would suit you better anyway. Competitions which depend on your inventiveness should never be sidestepped, for this is one of the ways in which you may just be able to fill up the family coffers. Your lucky periods are around your birthday, plus June and October.

Romantic Prospects 1992

Have you ever wondered why suddenly for no apparent reason you lose interest in love and in sex? No? Don't pretend that it never happens to you. Let me refresh that grey matter.

There you are after a couple of sexually, or romantically, hectic weeks considering applying for the lover-of-the-year award when, quite suddenly, the TV becomes more attractive than any member of the opposite sex you have seen for some time. Could it be connected with your birth sign? Yes, it most certainly can. Venus and Mars are the planets that count.

Favourably placed, they improve your looks, vitality and zest for living, but when they gang up on you, you have about as much confidence in yourself as King Kong at a beauty contest! Your nerves jangle and mentally, you are preoccupied with external matters. But not to worry, your sex appeal will return. It is simply a matter of time. The table opposite has been compiled in order to prepare you for your romantically active periods.

How to interpret the table

1 HEART – poor. If you try hard, someone of the opposite sex may decide to go out with you, but it is going to be hard work.
2 HEARTS – fair. If your lover has nothing better to do, then you may be lucky, but you will need to make the move.
3 HEARTS – good. Watch out, you are getting some mighty strange looks. Whoops! Well I did warn you! It is a pretty hot time.
4 HEARTS – wow! Take cover, unless you want to be caught in the stampede.

Your Romantic Prospects for 1992

	Jan	Feb	Mar	Apr	May	June	July	Aug	Sept	Oct	Nov	Dec
Aries	♥♥	♥	♥	♥♥♥♥	♥	♥	♥♥	♥♥	♥♥♥	♥	♥♥	♥♥
Taurus	♥♥	♥♥	♥	♥♥	♥♥♥♥	♥	♥♥	♥	♥♥♥	♥♥♥	♥♥	♥
Gemini	♥♥♥♥	♥♥	♥♥	♥	♥♥♥♥	♥♥♥♥	♥	♥♥	♥♥	♥♥♥	♥♥♥	♥
Cancer	♥	♥♥♥	♥♥	♥	♥	♥♥♥	♥♥♥	♥♥♥	♥♥	♥	♥♥♥	♥♥♥
Leo	♥♥	♥♥♥	♥♥	♥	♥♥	♥♥	♥♥♥	♥♥♥	♥♥	♥♥	♥	♥♥♥♥
Virgo	♥	♥♥	♥♥♥	♥♥♥	♥♥	♥	♥	♥	♥♥♥	♥	♥♥	♥
Libra	♥	♥	♥♥	♥♥	♥♥	♥	♥	♥	♥♥	♥♥	♥	♥♥
Scorpio	♥	♥	♥♥	♥	♥	♥	♥	♥♥	♥	♥	♥	♥
Sagittarius	♥♥♥♥♥	♥	♥♥♥♥	♥	♥	♥	♥♥♥	♥	♥♥♥	♥♥♥	♥♥♥	♥♥
Capricorn	♥♥	♥♥♥♥	♥♥	♥♥	♥♥	♥	♥♥♥	♥♥	♥♥	♥♥	♥♥♥	♥♥♥♥
Aquarius	♥	♥♥♥	♥♥♥♥	♥	♥	♥♥	♥♥♥	♥	♥	♥	♥	♥♥♥
Pisces	♥	♥	♥♥♥♥	♥♥	♥	♥♥	♥	♥♥♥	♥	♥♥	♥♥	♥

Health Year 1992

We all have our accident prone days. You know the kind of thing: you get out of bed and walk into the bedroom door, fall down the stairs, trip over the cat, burn your hands on the kettle and then, finally, as you rush out of the door to catch that important train you discover that it is Sunday! Does this sound familiar? Of course. There are also other days when, for no apparent reason, you wake up with nerves jangling. The slightest noise, like the rustle of a newspaper, and you are reaching for the tranquillizers! Could this have anything to do with astrology? Yes.

Each physical ailment is a symptom of a bad aspect from Mars, Venus, Jupiter, et cetera. The table opposite has been compiled in order for you to check out your bad weeks, and with any luck prepare for them.

How to interpret the table

THE HAMMER – This is the symbol of the headache. Possibly caused by tension, toothache or simply a hangover.

THE WARNING – Watch out – those nerves will be easily shredded. Put in your ear plugs and hope for the best.

BLACK CLOUD – Depression. There will be a tendency for you during this week to feel that the end of the world is nigh. Take constructive steps to keep yourself occupied.

BANDAGED FINGER – Accident prone. Anything from a cut finger to a sore heel.

THE APPLE – Relax – you are hale and hearty.

Your Health Year 1992

Marriage Year 1992

Marriage can be a pretty crazy business at the best of times, or should I say the worst? So, can astrology affect it? Yes. When a marriage comes under the influence of Venus, all in the Garden of Love is pink clouds and beautiful sunsets, but when Mars decides to oppose your marriage, watch out for fireworks. Getting on with your partner at this time can be something of a challenge.

The table opposite has been compiled in order to help you through the coming year. For let us not forget, prevention is often better than cure. If you know that your spouse is going to be in a touchy mood, then you can be extra loving, if you are wise. If you are not – don't say I didn't warn you!

How to interpret the table

THE BALLOON – Shows a week taken up with socializing which, for the most part, should be happy.

THE CLOCK – Watch out for boredom. It will eat away at your relationship, not to mention your brain!

THE HEART – This is fairly self-explanatory. Time for romance, soft lights, sweet music and an early night!

THE BOMB – Mars is acting against you. Therefore, you can expect arguments through tension and general dissatisfaction. If you want your relationship to last, you should be patient and extra loving during these weeks.

THE DOVE – A peaceful time.

Your Marriage Year 1992

	1st week	2nd week	3rd week	
Jan	balloon	balloon	dove	clock
Feb	bomb	bomb	balloon	heart
Mar	heart	balloon	dove	bomb
Apr	dove	clock	clock	dove
May	clock	balloon	dove	balloon
June	heart	balloon	heart	bomb
July	bomb	dove	heart	heart
Aug	balloon	bomb	clock	bomb
Sept	heart	heart	balloon	balloon
Oct	dove	clock	clock	bomb
Nov	heart	bomb	dove	dove
Dec	dove	heart	balloon	heart

r Sex Appeal

...lly attractive to the opposite sex and other ... a compelling determination and indomitable ... you like to take part in revolutionary causes? ... kind of genius for whatever it is you do? Are you in... n new inventions or original ideas? For the clues to this b... viour you should consult the planet Uranus. It is important for everyone who wants to foresee events and dominate their environment to understand the position of Uranus in their own particular horoscope.

Uranus in Aries

You have Uranus in Aries if you were born between the following dates:

31 March 1927 to 4 November 1927
13 January 1928 to 6 June 1934
10 October 1934 to 27 March 1935

Uranus in Aries gives the will to dominate and lead; there is great fire and independence of spirit. These individuals have an inner urge for supremacy, and they brook no opposition; when thwarted their tempers can be explosive. They consider it a positive affront when others differ with them and deal with such persons accordingly.

For such people, their will and their head are as one. They often have a fixed idea that is compatible with their inner drive, and if Uranus is in a strong position in their horoscope, they will concentrate all their forces on realizing their ambitions and convincing the world about their ideas. Nevertheless, while equally strong their will is not as consistent as Uranus in Capricorn and Taurus, since they become bored with a particular project for no apparent reason and then turn all their energy towards realizing some entirely different goal. This in turn may occupy them for some time, but they are likely to drop it just as suddenly.

Therefore, while possessing a certain enterprising spirit and true courage, it is hard for such people to build consistently. This characteristic gives them the ability to attract easily, but not to maintain interest in the opposite sex.

34

Famous people with this position:

Edward Kennedy   Anne Bancroft
Leslie Caron   Fidel Castro
Audrey Hepburn   Jaqueline Kennedy

Uranus in Taurus

You have Uranus in Taurus if you were born between the following dates:

6 June 1934 to 9 October 1934
27 March 1935 to 7 August 1941
5 October 1941 to 14 May 1942

Uranus in Taurus is a position *par excellence* for remarkable will-power and determination, the inner drive being expressed in the most positive ways. The desire is to build, but whether this is to further some high ideal or to achieve a more material goal depends on the rest of the horoscope. In some cases, this position can impart a magnetic and distinctive quality to the singing voice, and can be an asset for those who take up the acting profession. When afflicted, it can result in some irritation of the throat. Uranus gives a prodigious amount of energy and the will to act is monumental; this may account for Guy de Maupassant's extensive works, George Bernard Shaw's plays, Napoleon's urge to build empires and Sigmund Freud's labours on psychoanalysis. Such men are typical of the giants this placing of Uranus can produce.

Amongst the less famous, the position bestows great firmness, diligence and patience. There is also present a dogged determination to be constructive, whatever the field.

If your Sun is in Taurus, Virgo or Capricorn, then people will be attracted to you like flies; to some extent this may irritate you, for you do not always enjoy being the centre of attraction.

Famous people with this position:

Julie Christie   Julie Andrews
Jane Fonda   Connie Francis
George Bernard Shaw   John Lennon
Warren Beatty

Uranus in Gemini

You have Uranus in Gemini if you were born between the following dates:

8 August 1941 to 5 October 1941
14 May 1942 to 29 August 1948
12 November 1948 to 9 June 1949

It is through ideas rather than actions that you express your inner drive. Gentle and intellectual when it comes to persuading others to do your will, your strongest urges usually express themselves by means of the spoken and written word rather than through actual physical force. There are of course exceptions, such as Muhammad Ali, but even he exerted his will by the deft, rapid movements of his fists, which are ruled by Gemini. Gemini can also affect the voice and its magnetism in singers, actors or orators is evident. In art the expression can be linear and highly intellectual, as in the case of Toulouse-Lautrec.

If Uranus is badly aspected in your horoscope, you may be somewhat ineffectual in getting your own way, but when well-aspected you may express yourself successfully as a writer, teacher, journalist, lawyer, scientist, musician or in any occupation where cleverness with your mind, voice or fingers is important.

Famous people with this position:

Hayley Mills
Prince Charles
Brenda Lee
Mia Farrow

Geraldine Chaplin
Paul McCartney
George Harrison

Uranus in Cancer

You have Uranus in Cancer if you were born between the following dates:

30 August 1948 to 11 November 1948
20 June 1949 to 24 August 1955
28 January 1956 to 9 June 1956

Your deepest inner urges tend to be passive rather than active. You obey the dictates of your subconscious, and are sensitive and receptive rather than positive and strong-willed. In negative types this gives a very placid disposition; chameleon-like, these people assume the colours of their environment. Others can be highly developed on a psychic plane. With Uranus in Cancer will-power is not particularly aggressive, unless the Sun is in Taurus, Leo, Scorpio or Aquarius. Even when the Uranian traits of magnetism and will are fully developed, as in the case of Gandhi for example, leadership takes the form of passive resistance rather than openly declared war.

Among the less famous, there is a will to express themselves as gourmets, antique collectors or cooks. The men, as well as the women, have an urge to be homemakers and to mother the young, or they may desire to be mothered themselves and enjoy all the comforts of home. Many of you like to be popular, and you can be. In politics, literature or advertising you have the common touch, while in business you sense the public demand, especially when you deal in commodities for the home.

When Uranus is well-aspected, the artistic or musical sensibilities tend to be exquisite. When badly-aspected such people have explosive temperaments, disrupting their environments wilfully and arbitrarily. They are often a trial to their mothers in earlier years and subsequently disruptive in their own homes.

Famous people with this position:

Lord Byron   Henri Matisse
Bertrand Russell   Princess Anne

Uranus in Leo

You have Uranus in Leo if you were born between the following dates:

25 August 1955 to 27 January 1956
10 June 1956 to 1 November 1961
10 January 1962 to 9 August 1962

Uranus in this position, if afflicted, can bring trouble and obstacles to life, especially in youth: there will usually be some form of loss or privation, possibly through the father. These people display a disregard for convention, a great love of freedom and independence and a sometimes rebellious disposition, which can incur the dissatisfaction of superiors. Such individuals are fickle and changeable in love matters or, on the other hand, may suffer greatly from this trait in others.

Well-aspected, it is good for a public or professional career and much success may be achieved in this way. However, there may be social setbacks or annoyances, and hindrances through children. If your Sun is in Leo, Aries or Sagittarius then you have tremendous magnetism for others, but while you may bathe in the sunlight of popularity and carry a heavy engagement book you need to be far more cautious than other people when it comes to choosing a partner.

Famous people with this position:

John McEnroe
Princess Caroline of Monaco
Jenny Agutter
Tatum O'Neil

Uranus in Virgo

You have Uranus in Virgo if you were born between the following dates:

2 November 1961 to 9 January 1962
10 August 1962 to 23 June 1969

Uranus in Virgo makes you hyper-critical, and gives you unusual ideas about food and health which can lead to eccentric eating habits or 'quack cures', especially if this has been encouraged in early youth. However, it is an excellent placing for your intellectual ability and it is in fact through the mind that you attract other people. Lively, chatty and witty – ever ready with a clever retort – you are also subtle, penetrating, independent and original. You should succeed well in partnership or in association with other people.

Capricorns, Virgos and Taureans are strongly attracted to you physically. They may not necessarily be in the correct signs for marriage, but it is they who are drawn to you at the crook of your little finger.

Famous people with this position:

Tracy Austin	Lena Zavaroni
Brooke Shields	

Uranus in Libra

You have Uranus in Libra if you were born between the following dates:

29 September 1968 to 21 May 1969
29 June 1969 to 20 November 1974
2 May 1975 to 7 September 1975

With Uranus in Libra you are split by the need to be true to your individuality while remaining loyal to the demands of society and others. Your personal freedom is at stake, so make your position known. Struggle valiantly to combine the best of both worlds in order to compromise.

It is likely that you will become aware of the differences separating you from the generation that preceded you. By then you will have devised a new formula that will re-establish the necessary sovereignty of the family unit and its value in providing order and guidance in the lives of those being born.

There is tremendous power and magnetism in your personality which can attract at an alarming rate. When you marry you will decide to limit the size of your family, not only to ensure that it receives the attention it deserves but also to allow you to enjoy a greater freedom to find personal fulfilment, probably through creative outlets.

Famous people with this position:

Bros.

Uranus in Scorpio

You have Uranus in Scorpio if you were born between the following dates:

21 November 1974 to 1 May 1975
8 September 1975 to 16 February 1981
21 March 1981 to 15 November 1981

In this placing you are an extremely honest person, involved in the deeper subjects of existence such as death, sex and the spiritual continuity of life. Keen to learn all you can about everything, especially if it is considered taboo, you are unabashed and quite happy to ask questions because you do not fear the answers you may receive.

You are probably more aware of your spiritual commitment to others than those who profess to be but do not live up to their beliefs in terms of their actions. You have a personal, important destiny and it is on you that future generations will depend for the honesty that will allow the world to progress to new heights of awareness, enjoying a greater degree of development through personal and spiritual enlightenment.

On a more personal level you will quickly discover that other people are either fascinated – almost hypnotized – by you, or else totally repulsed. There will be no middle way, and this you must accept at an early age. To many, you are overwhelmingly irresistible. Make sure you do not misuse this wonderful gift.

Famous people with this position:

None to date.

Punters' Luck for 1992

Jockeys for the 1992 Flat Racing Season – Lucky Dates

Gambling is always a precarious business of course, and the following has been compiled in order to help the regular race-goer to minimize his or her losing bets.

The dates given are the good days shown on the jockey's birth chart.

CASH ASMUSSON March 31; April 1, 11, 12, 25; May 1, 6, 7, 14, 21–23 inclusive; June 1, 8, 9, 15, 18, 25; July 2, 3, 4, 6, 29, 30; August 3, 4, 7, 13, 21; September 3, 4, 16, 22, 28; October 4, 5, 10, 12, 17, 20, 23; November 3.

STEVE CAUTHEN March 24; April 6*, 7, 9*, 23, 25; May 4, 5, 7, 24, 25; June 2, 14, 25–27 inclusive, 30; July 1*, 2*, 17*, 18, 19, 22, 23, 26, 31; August 16, 26; September 3, 4, 7*, 8, 10, 22, 23, 25–28 inclusive; October 17 (early), 22; November 8.

RAY COCHRANE March 18, 20, 29; April 3, 16, 17*, 19; May 8*, 9, 26, 28*; June 3, 4, 13, 18*, 19; July 5, 8, 9*, 10, 11, 20*, 31*; August 4, 5, 6, 7*, 11*, 12, 28; September 10, 11, 20, 21*, 22; October 11, 21*, 23; November 1, 2, 5.

PAT EDDERY March 26, 28, 29*; April 9, 24; May 10, 14–17 inclusive, 21–23 inclusive; June 4, 10, 16, 25–27 inclusive; July 4*, 5, 6, 12, 22*; August 10*, 11, 12, 29, 30*; September 13, 30; October 13, 17; November 4*, 10, 13.

MICHAEL HILLS March 24–26 inclusive; April 3, 4, 5*, 8*, 10; May 9, 10, 11*, 21, 22; June 5*, 16, 20, 28, 29; July 6, 7*, 12*, 13*, 20, 23*; August 5*, 6, 13, 16–19 inclusive, 23; September 1, 2*, 7, 13, 15*, 16, 23; October 4, 6, 17, 18, 31; November 1, 4.

RICHARD HILLS March 28*; April 9*, 11*, 17 (late), 26; May 2, 12*, 23, 25; June 5, 12, 13, 17, 23, 30; July 3, 9–11 inclusive, 12*, 13, 14, 23, 30 (late); August 6, 14*, 15, 16, 18, 31; September 1, 14, 24, 28, 30; October 15, 17, 18*; November 5, 11.

RICHARD QUINN March 28, 31; April 9, 11, 16, 23, 27, 29, 30*; May 1, 4, 8, 11, 13, 25, 28, 31; June 1, 5, 8, 10, 14, 29; July 1, 2*, 3, 14, 15, 17, 23, 28*; August 2, 6, 8, 22, 28 (late); September 2, 3, (early), 14, 15*, 16, 17, 24, 25, 30*; October 7 (evening), 12*, 13–17 inclusive; November 12, 13.

JOHN REID March 20, 25; April 9, 13, 14*, 18; May 3, 4, 8, 11, 12, 29, 30; June 5 (early), 10, 17–19 inclusive, 30; July 1, 2, 12, 18, 27, 31; August 1*, 2, 4, 6, 14, 21; September 1*, 14, 19, 20; October 1*, 2*, 4, 8, 10*, 21, 28, 31; November 1*, 5–7 inclusive.

PAUL ROBINSON March 28, 29; April 6, 7, 9*, 17, 29; May 1, 6, 7, 10*, 21*, 27, 29*; June 4, 7, 10, 13, 16, 27, 29; July 1, 2, 3*, 6, 8, 11, 12*, 15; August 4, 9, 11, 12*, 13, 14, 29, 31*; September 3, 9, 12, 15, 23, 28, 29; October 9, 13, 17, 25; November 3, 7.

WALTER SWINBURN March 7, 25, 31; April 10*, 12–15 inclusive, 28, 30; May 7*, 10, 16*, 17, 25, 26, 30; June 5, 6*, 11, 12, 16, 19, 20, 26*; July 1, 15, 16, 23*; August 1, 9, 17, 19, 25*; September 3*, 7, 13, 22, 25*, 26*, 27*; October 4, 8, 21, 22, 25, 27, 28; November 1, 6*, 7.

Trainers for the 1992 Flat Racing Season – Lucky Dates

The following dates could be particularly useful when combined with those previously given for the jockeys.

LESTER PIGGOT March 16, 17*, 23, 30; April 2*, 9*, 16, 17*, 21, 28, 30*; May 1*, 3, 9, 17*, 24, 27*, 29; June 2, 13, 17*, 19, 21*, 22, 24, 25, 27*; July 4, 5, 14, 16, 19, 20, 22*, 26, 29; August 11*, 13, 16*, 18; September 10, 11, 19*, 20, 26, 28*, 29; October 3*, 4, 5, 20*, 24, 28; November 3*.

CLIVE BRITTAIN March 14, 26, 29; April 6, 8, 9*, 10, 11, 24; May 7–10 inclusive, 16, 20, 30*, 31; June 1, 4, 10, 22, 27, 28; July 6, 11*, 21*, 22*, 23*, 24; August 4*, 29; September 1, 2, 4, 5*, 22; October 1–4 inclusive, 12*, 16*, 30, 31; November 6–8 inclusive.

NEVILLE CALLAGHAN March 26, 29*; April 6, 7*, 9, 24; May 18, 21, 22; June 26, 27, 30; July 1, 2, 3*, 11, 12*, 20; August 5*, 12–17 inclusive, 29, 30; September 11*, 12–14 inclusive; October 7, 8, 13, 16*, 17, 28–30 inclusive; November 1*, 4, 9, 12.

HENRY CECIL March 23, 27, 31; April 8, 10, 25*, 26; May 10, 11, 19, 21; June 18, 26, 27; July 4–7 inclusive, 12, 13*, 14; August 5, 6, 13, 14, 28; September 4, 5, 23, 25; October 1–4 inclusive, 13, 16; November 4, 10, 11.

GUY HARWOOD March 20, 25, 26, 29; April 5, 10, 15, 17, 23; May 10, 11, 15, 16*, 24; June 9*, 13, 22, 27; July 10, 14, 20, 22*, 26, 28, 30; August 11, 12, 14, 16–18 inclusive, 20, 26, 28; September 5, 11*, 12, 13, 15, 18, 26, 28*; October 11, 12*, 13, 15, 16*, 18, 21, 27, 28; November 3, 9, 10.

BARRY HILLS March 24, 25, 28; April 7, 25*, 26, 30; May 1, 6, 14*, 19, 22; June 2, 3*, 6, 13, 17, 19, 28, 30; July 3, 12, 14, 15, 23, 25, 28; August 2, 6, 9, 10*, 11, 20, 23, 27, 28*, 30; September 1, 5, 10, 11*, 13, 20, 28, 29; October 5, 8, 10*, 18, 22, 26, 28, 29*; November 3*, 9.

FULKE JOHNSON-HOUGHTON March 21; April 1, 4, 6, 20, 21*; May 4*, 12, 21*, 30; June 1, 4, 6, 12, 17, 22, 24, 25, 27; July 12, 13, 23*; August 14*, 16, 18–20 inclusive, 21*, 22, 31; September 1, 7, 14, 23, 24; October 1, 5, 18, 23–25 inclusive; November 5, 11.

DAVID O'BRIEN March 19; April 2 (late), 3*, 4, 17, 18; May 1*, 5 (early), 10 (early), 18, 27, 28*; June 4, 5, 10*, 16, 18, 19, 22, 23, 26; July 9, 10*, 20, 27; August 20, 26, 27; September 2, 3*, 4, 5, 20, 29; October 21*, 23, 27; November 9–11 inclusive.

MICHAEL STOUTE March 21, 24, 25*; April 5, 6, 17, 24–27 inclusive; May 7, 10, 14*, 21, 23, 25, 26; June 6*, 14, 25, 26, 28; July 14, 17–19 inclusive, 23*, 27; August 1, 5, 9, 27; September 8, 9*, 10*, 27*; October 8, 23, 24, 25*, 26*, 27, 28; November 3.

JOHN SUTCLIFFE March 23*, 28; April 5, 8, 22*, 23; May 6, 23, 28; June 2, 3*, 13, 16 (late); July 13*, 16*, 25, 31 (evening);

August 15*, 24, 25, 28*, 29*, 30, 31; September 1, 5, 6, 20, 25; October 7, 15, 16*, 26, 27*; November 3, 8 (early), 9.

These dates are especially good.

The Year in Focus

As an Aquarius subject, you are the most determined and independent of persons. You can be obstinate, headstrong and perverse too. Nobody who has this sign strong in their charts likes to be pinned down to intimate personal relationships for longer than they feel such a state of affairs is a personal need. You are like a horse that must be ridden on a loose rein. So long as you feel that you are making the decisions and working to your own method, all is well – but a hint of coercion, and you turn into a rebel. This character analysis is necessary due to the fact that Saturn (the disciplinarian) continues in your sign. Therefore, like it or not you cannot be as free-wheeling as you would generally wish. The stars are attempting to teach you self-discipline, responsibility and all those boring things you spend most of your time avoiding. However, if you rebel it will be extremely hard for you, so try to accept that life necessitates hard work and a more sober outlook. Remember too that this planet rules falls, bruises and dental problems, so look after yourself in all these areas.

Having looked at the deficit side, now let's consider the credit aspect. Lucky Jupiter stays in Virgo until October; up until this time therefore your opportunities will come through those in big business, insurance, mortgage companies and the bank manager. Just for once, the latter will be prepared to support some of your ideas, provided they are presented sensibly.

From October onwards, though, Jupiter moves into Libra and this brings good fortune through matters related to abroad, further education and legal affairs. Uranus and Neptune continue in your solar twelfth house, and there will be times when uncertainty dogs your every step – not that outward appearances would indicate anything of this nature. When feelings of insecurity descend without logical reason, blame it on the stars. Pluto continues to wend its way through the zenith of your chart creating sudden beginnings and endings and a degree of upheaval where professional matters are concerned. But you are the type to thrive on change, so there is nothing to fear in this direction.

Romantically, there will be times when you feel inclined to settle down, and these will be dealt with in the month-to-month guide. Financially, it will pay you to indulge in a small amount of research; rooting around in the background of deals or situations will throw up information which can lead to profit. Now for a deeper look at the year ahead.

January

With five planets leaping around in Capricorn – the part of your chart devoted to your subconscious – it is likely that you are suffering from a good deal of inner turmoil and may not be feeling at one with your surroundings. However, now that you have been warned you should learn to patronize yourself and get on with life. On a professional level this month favours those involved in research or work that could be described as being behind the scenes – such as wardrobe mistress, sleeping partners in business, financiers and the medical profession. Also a good time for other Aquarians needing to deal with such matters.

Socially there is plenty of action, most of it with friends or within a club. If you are single when romance comes your way, it is likely to blossom under such circumstances. So take care during the last week of the month. Someone of the opposite sex is not being strictly honest with you, and as you are the truth-teller of the Zodiac, subterfuge is hard for you to digest. So be careful. Healthwise, providing you have visited the dentist as suggested, there should be little for you to complain about. But ignore this advice and there could be problems later in the year. Financially, what you overhear or inadvertently see could lead to profit in some way. However, it is not the best time in your life for taking mad chances – bear this in mind.

The New Moon on the 4th in Capricorn brings to the surface situations that were previously hidden; suddenly you are confronted with them and decisions are necessary. The Full Moon in Leo on the 21st makes it the worst possible day for being too pushy where other people are concerned; the end of a relationship could be the result. Further, circumstances in a partnership could be changing, and you may find it hard to adapt to this.

February

This is your time of the year, so it is a good month for pushing ahead with all matters of self-interest. Mercury joins the Sun in your sign, making it an ideal time for freelances or home workers. It is also favourable if you are involved in travel, the literary world, or professionally employed in an old family concern. Whatever your aims in life, now is the time to gather your courage in both hands and push forward; you could do well.

Socially and romantically life is rather quiet until the 18th. Where love affairs are concerned, life could be unbelievably complicated until this date, and ideally the people who enter your life early in the month should not be taken too seriously. However, once Venus and Mars enter your sign after the 18th you are positively irresistible: confident, at your most charming, passionate and enterprising. What more could anyone ask? If you have decided to get married late in the month, then you have been extremely clever. The single who are hoping to find the ideal partner may just strike lucky, so do get out and circulate after mid-month. There will certainly be plenty of opportunities, so make sure you snap them up.

Financially the first couple of weeks seem to be the most important. There are genuine offers and the possible chance of a new career. Don't be slow, say 'Yes' in a loud voice. On the health front, over-indulgence and a certain tendency to be accident-prone through haste are indicated in the last couple of weeks, but this pitfall aside you are in A1 condition.

The New Moon in your sign on the 3rd hails new beginning of some description; it is certainly a time for exploring fresh pastures in all areas of life. The Full Moon in opposition around the 18th suggests either changes in circumstances in a relationship, which you must adapt to, or the possibility of hidden grievances coming to the surface.

March

This is a great time for those involved in the money professions such as accountants, bankers, financiers and brokers etc. For all, now is always the time of year when you concentrate on the financial areas of life, and goodness knows you need at least a month in order to do so! So now you must confront those brown envelopes and try to sort out your complicated affairs. However, at least this year you get a little help from Venus; after the 14th it enters Pisces and should bring with it some opportunities for you to swell the bank balance. True, you may be putting a lot of effort into changing your image or perhaps improving your home, but somehow you will manage to end this month richer than when it began.

Socially and romantically, Venus and Mars squat in your sign until mid-month. You are at your most compelling and magnetic then, so it's relatively easy to get your own way in all areas. Also good if you have decided to get married at this time. Regrettably, the presence of Mars in your sign for the entire month could lead to an erratic flow of energy: one minute you are full of beans, the next you are exhausted. A certain tendency to be accident-prone is indicated too, so control haste and be scrupulous with your food and drink intake.

Mercury's position in Aries suggests numerous opportunities for you to get out and about; a restless mood descends and you need plenty to occupy your mind. The New Moon on the 4th in Pisces indicates a fresh source of income, so it is a great time for job interviews. The Full Moon in Virgo on the 18th advises you to steer clear of important negotiations or confrontations with bureaucracy, officialdom or the bank manager. You could finish up all the poorer if you are too daring on this particular day.

April

This is a good month for you as if offers a certain amount of variety, to-ing and fro-ing and activity. It favours those professionally involved in the media, transport, communications advertising and sales. Any chances to go on business trips should be snapped up. The emphasis also seems to be on the affairs of in-laws or brothers and sisters, and they will be taking up a good deal of your time. At a financial level Mars has entered the money area of your chart, encouraging impulse in this direction; so for goodness' sake steer clear of the stores, unless you are shopping for necessities.

Romantically, Venus enters Aries on the 7th, bringing the chance of many brief encounters. Don't expect anything world-shattering, it is definitely better to play the field – but often that is the way you prefer it to be anyway. Healthwise, there are few problems unless you count the occasional hangover or minor stomach upset – nothing serious to worry you.

The New Moon on the 7th in Gemini points to an exciting invitation. For parents, there may be decisions which have to be taken on behalf of offspring. Romance too is a strong possibility. The Full Moon in Libra on the 17th advises you to stay clear of lawyers and those in education, also if possible to avoid long-distance travel where complication is likely to be the order of the day.

May

On a financial level, Mars continues in the money area of your chart, therefore you will still be inclined to throw your money around as if you have just printed it. This is sure to have a bad effect on your life at a later date unless you get it under control fast. At a professional level, so much activity in Taurus bodes well for those involved in family concerns, property and the allied trades.

It is quite likely than until the 25th you will be happy within the confines of your home, acting as host/hostess rather than in the role of guest. Plenty of activity in your own environment suggests that there are some home improvements going on in there somewhere. The best time for romance and generally having fun is after the 25th, when you become more adventurous and are ready to circulate once more. Healthwise, there is little to mar your month and you should be in fine fettle. Financially any offers that come in after the 21st should be seriously considered.

The New Moon this months falls on the 2nd in the property and domestic area of your chart, so you can expect changes in this direction. The Full Moon on the 16th occupies the zenith of your chart and could mean the end of a cycle in some sphere connected with professional matters. It is not a time to be too pushy with work colleagues or superiors.

June

Mars' position in Aries for the first two weeks of this month suggests that you should be more cautious on the roads, and remember that other people have the right to be there too. And even if you are extra careful, bear in mind that there is always some fool lurking around the corner. If you are going to have any problems this June they will be caused by traffic. That is until after the 15th when Mars moves into Taurus, at which point your family could be decidedly awkward and tense. Property matters are not well-starred either, so don't push in this direction.

Professionally speaking it is those who are involved in the arts, sport, entertainment, animals and children who will fare best. Promotion or more money are expected for these Aquarians. Romantically and socially, the first three weeks are considerably hectic and there will be many opportunities for romancing and generally having fun – though don't take anything that happens on an emotional level too seriously. Your judgement is totally lacking where the opposite sex is concerned, so content yourself with having a good time rather than making any heavy commitment. Financially you should take particular care late in the month when you will be tempted to spend in order to impress. Don't bother, this simply won't work – just be yourself.

The 1st is New Moon day and it falls in Gemini. If you should have the good fortune to be planning something special on a social or romantic level, it should go with a swing. Also a good time for making personal changes. Full Moon on the 15th in Sagittarius suggests you tread carefully when in the company of friends; it won't take much to give offence, and you could lose an old and much valued friend.

July

Mars continues in the domestic, family and property area of your chart until the 27th, so there a good deal of tension is evident. Don't make it worse by being too opinionated, insisting on always having your own way, or maintaining that you are always right. On a professional level, it's those involved in the medical profession, health matters or the service industries who seem likely to do best. Office workers also do well, and there may be news of a rise or some promotion. Now is a great time of the year for hiring the skills and talents of other people if necessary – you will get good value. For Aquarians the atmosphere with colleagues should be somewhat improved at work, with others being cooperative for a change. If you are going on holiday then hopefully you are leaving early in the month, as there could be delays and a few problems later on.

On a romantic and social level, remember that other people will have better ideas on how to have fun than you, so just for once be prepared to play the sporting role and go along with them. Those who are getting engaged or married after the 16th could not have picked a better time. For the single, the best time for meeting 'that special someone' is after the 14th, so don't sit at home feeling sorry for yourself but get out and circulate – it's the only way. Healthwise, early in the month you may be suffering from the effects of over-indulgence or exhaustion, but this wears off as time progresses.

The Full Moon this month falls on the 14th, a day when you are feeling rather insecure and give full rein to fears and phobias. Adopt a patronizing attitude towards yourself, do nothing important and all will be well. The New Moon on the 29th in Leo brings a fresh set of circumstances in an existing relationship, or conversely someone new and exciting comes into your life. All in all not a bad month, but you may have to pick your way through the dodgier aspects.

August

This is the time of year when you need to shelve your independent streak and be prepared to play a supporting role and give encouragement to other people. If you form a professional partnership during this month it will certainly be well-starred. Further, it is a good time for those who act as agents or managers, since business should be brisk. On a romantic level the first week is the most important, especially if you are getting engaged or married; the same applies to Aquarians going on holiday. After this date you become more introspective and channel your energies into domestic or professional affairs – being disinclined to 'waste time', as you call it, on the more frivolous sides to life.

Late month is a great time for approaching the bank manager, sorting out your complicated tax affairs or dealing with bureaucracy; unfortunately this will be necessary at some stage. Sportsmen should take care, for Mars' move into Gemini means that strains and sprains are the order of the day. Exhaustion and nerves could also plague on occasions, and you need to spoil yourself just a little during this month. Financially, provided you are prepared to make a few concessions you can get a pet project of yours off the ground. Money that is owed rolls in, but now is not a time for speculation.

The Full Moon in Pisces on the 14th suggests the conclusion of a cycle in connection with financial matters. Maybe a contract has come to an end, or possibly you may lose a prize possession. Keep your wits about you. The New Moon on the 28th in Virgo makes it a propitious time for chats with your bank manager, accountant or anyone in the money sphere in general. Certainly it is great for starting fresh work and good for job interviews too.

September

Many of you will consider this a rather boring month, but it is a good one for those professionally involved in finance, the Stock Exchange and big business in general. For other Aquarians it is certainly a favourable time for chats with your bank manager, who will give you support over a pet scheme of yours. However, you need to take care during the last two weeks of the month since Mars enters Cancer at this time and the atmosphere at work could become quite tense. Do not involve yourself with any petty squabbles or back-stabbing – keep yourself detached, it's the only way to go.

During the first two weeks of the month, yet again you are accident-prone where sporting activities are concerned. Be a spectator rather than a participator, for once. On the emotional level, it is a great time for those who have decided to take a late holiday; foreign admirers will be queuing up for your attention, while delays and complications are minimized for once. If you are at home, you will need to be a little less idealistic when it comes to the opposite sex and to take off the rose-coloured spectacles. Involvement with a foreigner is likely, as you are attracted to those who come from backgrounds differing from your own. During the last week there is a good deal of socializing going on in connection with work, and it is especially a favourable period for those in the luxury trades or the arts. Healthwise, watch out for strain during the last two weeks apart, but from this you should be in fine fettle.

The Full Moon in Cancer on the 12th signifies the end of a cycle in connection with work affairs or perhaps colleagues. The New Moon on the 26th makes it ideal for long-distance travel, and for dealing with lawyers or those in education. There are plenty of good ideas around at this time, but make sure you get them down on paper and do something about them other than talking. A relatively good month, all in all.

October

Regrettably Mars stays in Cancer for the remainder of 1992, therefore the tension at work will continue and the work-load will remain unusually heavy. You will need to set aside some time for putting your feet up if you are to get through the rest of the year; exhaustion can take its toll. On the professional level, now is the most wonderful time for those involved in the law, education or foreign affairs. Also good if you have decided to take an autumn break; you will thoroughly enjoy yourself, and complications will be minimal when it comes to travelling.

Jupiter has moved into Libra, which means that from now on you enter a twelve-month period when your good fortune can be located in connection with foreign, educational or legal affairs. Bear this in mind and be ready to snap up all opportunities. Romantically it's all somewhat boring, unfortunately, as opportunities for fun are confined to your work environment – great of course if you happen to have a crush on a colleague, but otherwise a little disappointing. The best thing to do is accept all invitations which come to you from associates; you won't be sorry. Healthwise, you can remain in A1 condition provided you ensure that you get plenty of rest.

The Full Moon in Aries on the 11th warns you to take care when travelling; you may be an excellent driver, but there are plenty of fools who are not! Try to be a little more tactful when dealing with relatives, particularly in-laws. The New Moon on the 25th occurs at the zenith of your chart, making it a wonderful time for interviews, negotiations or presenting ideas. A minor new cycle is about to begin in your professional life.

November

By now you must be getting used to the rather disagreeable atmosphere at work, but before you hand in your resignation you would be well advised to see the year out and make absolutely certain that when you do leave you have something else to go to. This month is the most ambitious part of the year, when you will be pushing your way up the ladder of success and crawling over a few people in order to do so. This will not make you popular with loved ones – who will be feeling neglected – or with the colleagues whom you crush. Nevertheless it is a

53

great time if you happen to be a freelance worker, or involved in the literary business or travel; all can be highly successful.

Financially, the month improves as it progresses and there is sure to be a financial offer later in the month, so be ready to recognize it and act. Socially the action is to be found at clubs or with friends, and the same can be said where romance is concerned. Don't take the latter too seriously, though, it's really not going anywhere, so simply let down your hair and avoid being too intense. Provided you remain your usual Aquarian self, all should be well.

The Full Moon this month falls in Taurus on the 10th, suggesting the end of a cycle in connection with domestic, property or family affairs. The New Moon on the 24th in Sagittarius promises a fresh set of friends – perhaps met or introduced at a club. You will enjoy their lively and stimulating company, and this will provide your social life with a shot in the arm for the remainder of the year.

December

On a professional level the month favours those who work as members of a team or in administration. However, it will pay all Aquarians to root around in the background of things; you will be surprised what you can turn up, which will help you to make a professional decision.

Romantically, Venus is in your solar twelfth house during the first ten days. This is bad news, as it seems to suggest that other people are being anything but honest with you – and how you hate deception. It would be wise to check out all would-be admirers and make sure they are not already committed elsewhere. Once the 10th is past, all is sweetness and light. Venus is in your sign and you physically and mentally blossom; therefore a great time for a winter wedding or engagement. The single could very well meet someone special at one of those Christmas parties, in which case the relationship will be long-lived. Socially you are in great demand, and there is no need to pick up the phone in order to make arrangements; on the contrary, you will find it difficult to fit everybody into your diary. Financially, the best period in the month is the first nine days, when you should be sure to do all you can to generate cash – you will certainly need it at this time of the year. Healthwise, apart from the usual risk of over-indulgence all should be well.

The Full Moon on the 9th in Gemini suggests that a social occasion to which you are looking forward either will not come up to your expectations or else may be cancelled altogether. Never mind, there is plenty of fun and games to be had elsewhere. The New Moon in Capricorn on the 24th is a clear indication that for once you should trust to your intuitions and 'gut feelings' rather than logic. You will find this pays you well. By the end of this year, you will have decided that you have learned a lot, developed considerably and are looking forward to the New Year in an optimistic frame of mind.

Day-by-day Horoscope

January

1st – It is highly unlikely that you will be suffering from a hangover, although you may be feeling somewhat depressed. Try to find things to do that will occupy your intellect. Partners will still be celebrating this evening.

2nd – A good day for any business transactions, especially those which have been neglected in the past. Those working with, or for, foreigners will have a difficult time, misunderstandings being inevitable.

3rd – You will be counting the cost of the festive celebrations when a large bill is presented for payment. While you may be able to stall for a couple of days, it is advisable to pay up as soon as possible.

4th – This is the day of the New Moon, therefore it's a great time for beginning anything new – and that includes relationships. There is a chance to join in an unusual leisure-time activity; when it presents itself, accept.

5th – Romance for the single is badly-starred and it looks as if a relationship is coming to an end. Do not stay around where you are not wanted. This is a very happy evening for those who are married.

6th – Financial gains are probable, but only for those who have put in some hard work over the past months. Unexpected windfalls are not likely. This evening is a very good time for home entertaining.

7th – Let friends or partners make the entertainment plans, as your ideas will not be worth considering. Those staying at home find it is an ideal time for catching up on neglected correspondence.

8th – Not a good time for making professional or personal visits. Even those who have been neglected for some time will not be pleased to see you. Take the opportunity to make some long-term career or domestic plans.

9th – Not a good time for travelling, therefore you would be advised to curb the urge to get out and about. Business carried on from your home will be the most successful. Financial losses are indicated this evening.

10th – No need to get hot under the collar with colleagues who do not come up to your high standards today. They will have a perfectly valid reason if only you take the trouble to find out what it is.

11th – Try to be a little more practical today; your dreams are too unrealistic. Good ideas will come to you, but you will have to sift the wheat from the chaff. Be practical where romance is concerned too.

12th – Singles should not take romantic encounters too seriously – nor any promises that are made on the spur of the moment. This afternoon is the best time for quarrying an elusive friend or neighbour.

13th – The day is good for immediate action where ideas are concerned. Those that appeal to you most should be acted upon. Long-term plans can also be put into action now.

14th – Today it is what others are doing that will interest you; try to get yourself in on their plans. This afternoon is a good time for taking part in celebrations of all descriptions.

15th – Get away from the house for a few minutes today in order to blow the cobwebs away. Partners will be cooperative and understanding, so little explanation for your action will be needed.

16th – A good day for getting projects under way, especially if you have the support and backing of superiors. Colleagues will be less obstructive but still very unhelpful.

17th – Various members of the family will cause trouble; try to steer clear of them. Those working at home will be subject to interruptions and interference from partners.

18th – Headaches, hangovers and dizzy spells will be your main enemies today, so you should not attempt any DIY work around the house. Your concentration is totally lacking. Avoid handling any kind of complicated apparatus. Plan a relaxing day.

19th – Tiredness and a sense of getting nowhere will ruin a day full of social opportunities. Try to fight off your feelings of frustration in order to take advantage of prevailing conditions.

20th – A good day for dealing with officialdom and bureaucracy in all its guises. Adopting a more aggressive attitude towards those who are on your back will serve you well for a change.

21st – Those thinking of visiting relatives at a long distance are advised that travel is badly aspected, especially if going under your own steam; better to use public transport – and even that's not reliable.

22nd – Neighbours and colleagues make good entertainment partners. The single could very well be meeting someone special at a social event, so keep your eyes and ears open. A foreigner may feature in the day.

23rd – Give and take will be your watchword if you are dealing with older, cantankerous people. They will need to be given the benefit of the doubt on more than one occasion. The same is true of older relatives.

24th – Something of value which has been hidden away for some time may come to light; also, a financial offer made some while ago could come to fruition. Whichever way things happen you will benefit considerably.

25th – Make arrangements for short journeys early in the day and carry them through. Long-distance travel is not so well-aspected and delays will lead to disappointment and cancelled meetings.

26th – A lot of information can be gleaned from friends and lovers today. You may have to do some digging, but what you find out will be useful and illuminating. Try to keep expenditure on the evening's entertainment down to a minimum.

27th – A good day for having discussions in confidence with superiors. Career problems and fears can be aired and help will be given where it is asked for. This afternoon is important for long-distance communications.

28th – Married Aquarians will be finding their partners are going through a rather dull and boring state, and are advised to find something stimulating to compensate for this. This evening is a good time to join friends on an expedition of some description.

29th – Mercury moves into your sign, therefore a lucky few weeks lie ahead for those involved with travel, communications and the literary world. You take on new interests and it is a great time to embark on a fresh diet or health regime.

30th – Make your presence felt from the word go. Other people will be willing to listen to your ideas and digest your opinions, so this is the time for putting yourself in the limelight and blowing your own trumpet.

31st – You will find it extremely difficult to reach decisions regarding your career and, in some cases, your domestic life. You should seek advice from an experienced member of your family, therefore.

February

1st – A quiet start to the month. Others may feel like painting the town all shades of red, but you are in rather a subdued mood, preferring to read a good book or put your feet up in front of the television. Some resentment could occur because of this.

2nd – Someone you have not expected to see for some time will make an appearance, and you will be delighted. An unexpected gift will also come your way. Those about you will be behaving totally out of character – for good and bad.

3rd – This is the day of the New Moon and it falls in your sign. Therefore, you can expect a minor new cycle to begin within the next few days, perhaps in connection with your domestic, family or property affairs.

4th – A quiet day that should be spent in the company of those who stimulate you on an intellectual level. This is not the time for physical effort; you simply don't have the energy. A period of study may appeal to some.

5th – Home entertaining will be especially successful today. Try to mix business with pleasure whenever possible. Superiors will be willing to visit you in your home. This evening is an excellent time for those in love.

6th – Minor health problems could affect you, and along with a minor depression could lead to your having a rather bad day. However, things will brighten up this evening, thanks to the company of friends.

7th – A good day for making long-term career plans. You will need to explain your actions to other people so that they do not get insecure. This evening is a good time for married couples.

8th – Do not allow other people to dictate the pace of the day. Set yourself a target and work towards it steadily. However, do allow yourself a period for socializing; this afternoon is the best time for getting out and about for the sake of enjoyment.

9th – Financially you are likely to make some gains and some losses today. Care should be taken when spending cash on essential items, as you are likely to be taken for a ride. Loved ones are difficult to handle this evening.

10th – A good day for all those travelling in the course of their business. New contacts can be made who will be important to you in the future. This evening is the best time for getting together with superiors.

11th – If at all possible, the day should be spent away from home. But if this is not feasible, you will have to make do with what entertainment you make for yourself – and this could be rather expensive. A routine day at work.

12th – Try to get lovers to see your point of view when differences of opinion arise. Arguments are inevitable, but need not be too bitter. Plan an early night – friends should be dissuaded from visiting.

13th – If you are involved in a job which requires attention to detail and concentrated effort, then you are in for a good day. Your intuition and judgement are very well tuned and you will see through many people.

14th – Those working from home will be subject to interruption and delay, but there is little you can do about it. Make the most of the time available to you. A Cancerian may be occupying your thoughts.

15th – A good day for gamblers, when Lady Luck appears to be on your side. People with cash at risk will hear of good dividends. This afternoon is a favourable time for becoming involved with the ideas of another person, perhaps a friend.

16th – Many of you will begin to feel the pressure of an emotional problem. Someone is attempting to pin you down, and you may have to exit from the relationship in double-quick time. You are in no mood to make decisions. It is not a day to take work home; this will make you unpopular with the family.

17th – Mercury is now in the financial area of your chart, so during the next few weeks there may be gains in connection with travel or a contract. Keep your eyes and ears open.

18th – Full Moon today falls in your opposition, so take care when dealing with other people: they will be touchy. The best thing you can do is to be as independent as possible.

19th – Hidden feelings in a relationship begin to surface today, and you may not like what you see or hear. For the single, there may be an end of what appeared to be a promising affair.

20th – You will probably have to change your opinions about a work colleague due to his or her actions. Do no let this come as a surprise to you. This is a day when many people will be surprising you with their actions.

21st – Changes will have to be made in your routine in order to get through the day unscathed. What at first seems simple will become more complicated as you get into it, while the opposite is true of what appears difficult.

22nd – You could be reacting too violently to other people's comments; try to keep your temper under control. Your emotions will be bare this evening when a loved one upsets you; just for once you lose your cóol.

23rd – Tiredness could lead you to make some silly mistakes, and these will be costly in terms of both finance and in time. Best not to do any DIY, but leave it to the experts. Get out this evening with friends.

24th – You will be doing things on the spur of the moment today, so you will have to remain flexible. Do not make any hard and fast decisions, for they will have to be changed at the last minute. Travellers will find themselves being delayed at every twist and turn.

25th – Give the benefit of the doubt to younger people today; their ideas may not match your own, but at least they will be more sound. Don't rely on your own judgement of character; today you will be wrong.

26th – It appears that a loved one is trying to force your hand over a domestic matter. Do not allow this to happen. Married Aquarius subjects should not let their emotions get out of hand when dealing with a member of the opposite sex.

27th – A good day for making plans, but not for putting them into operation. Consultations about your career will have to wait, as superiors are in no mood to deal with them at present.

28th – Older work colleagues will have some good advice for you and you are advised to act on it. Financial losses are indicated this afternoon for housewives out shopping – carelessness being the main cause.

29th – The month goes out on a high note. You will have more energy than of late and will be able to deal with jobs that much more quickly.

March

1st – With Mars continuing in your sign, care should be taken where food and drink are concerned as there is a possibility of minor stomach complaints. Financially, this could be a rewarding day for the gambler.

2nd – The week begins on a high note for those connected with import/export or having foreign connections. Gains may be made in this area. Personal mail should be attended to, and nothing should be left to chance.

3rd – A good day for Aquarians away from home. You will get a lot of pleasure from joining in with friends and relatives. Those connected with sport should have a fulfilling and profitable time.

4th – This is the day of the New Moon and a time when you should be listening to your instincts, hunches and intuitions rather than your logical brain. Try it; you will be surprised at the results.

5th – Start the day as you mean to carry on. This is a time when you should be making your presence felt at your work-place, though not by pushing yourself to the head of the queue. Subtlety should be your watchword.

6th – Romance is in the air for those who are single. It is likely that a new a partner will be found at your place of work. Do not allow relatives to put upon you this evening.

7th – Give younger relatives a helping hand if they need it. You will benefit from having them on your side in the weeks to come. A good time will be had this evening if you are in the company of work colleagues.

8th – Dental problems could raise their heads today; if so, take time off to make an appointment with the dentist. Financially speaking this is not a lucky day, therefore you are advised against putting money at risk.

9th – Older members of this sign and Aquarians confined to home should benefit from a surprise letter or visit today. Those working behind the scenes or in research will also have a beneficial time.

10th – The indications are that many of you will be working in and around the home while trying to add value to your surroundings. The family can be enlisted to give help wherever possible.

11th – Be careful with whom you flirt today, as there is a likelihood of your getting into hot water. Those who are married should also take care when mixing with members of the opposite sex – your intentions could be misconstrued.

12th – A happy day at work, when all goes according to plan. The only place where friction could occur, however, is in your personal life, especially if you are married. Keep a guard on your tongue.

13th – Do not allow other people to steal your thunder; this is a day when you should take credit for your efforts. This afternoon is a good time for dealing with business correspondence and telephone calls.

14th – Venus enters the financial area of your chart today, so be alert over the coming weeks for opportunities to swell your purse or wallet. An especially good time for the artist or those in the luxury trades.

15th – If you want any kind of support – financial or otherwise – now is a good time to ask relatives and loved ones. You will experience many surprises and displays of consideration over the next few weeks.

16th – Those travelling for a living are advised to double-check all arrangements as it is likely you will end up in the wrong place at the wrong time. Stay at home this evening if you wish to save money.

17th – A good day for catching up on all those personal matters you have left unattended for some time – correspondence, telephone calls, etc. Those working in the home will find things running smoothly.

18th – This is the day of the Full Moon, so it is not a time to pay visits to bureaucrats, officials or the bank manager. You can expect no favours. Round off work already started rather than beginning anything new.

19th – Work colleagues who have been trying to undermine you for some time will come round to your way of thinking. Superiors and those in official positions will offer you a helping hand.

20th – A financial windfall is likely for those connected with the entertainment industry. A contract signed will offer you more than you had expected. Plan a quiet evening.

21st – Not a good day for putting any new experiment into operation; hold back until a more favourable time. Those who work from home could find that many interruptions delay progress. Friends and neighbours are in a sociable mood, so try to give them a warm welcome.

22nd – If out and about today, take care when dealing with the forces of law and order. You are likely to collect parking tickets etc. This afternoon is best for catching up on routine matters.

23rd – An interesting piece of news will come your way, and this will set you thinking about the future. A neighbour could impart some juicy scandal, but nothing you hear should be repeated.

24th – Collect your family about you today, and have an outing of some kind. Friends will be spoiling for an argument, so you would do well to steer clear of their company until this evening.

25th – Give and take is the order of the day. Allow younger people to have their say in whatever is planned for the day's activities. This afternoon will see friends dropping in for a serious chat.

26th – Get off to a good start this morning. Clear out all the dead wood from your work, and put finishing touches to routine matters. This afternoon is a favourable time for making long-term career decisions.

27th – Romance could be on the minds of single members of this sign, but care should be taken when chatting up older, more experienced members of the opposite sex. Entertainment will be expensive this evening.

28th – Mars enters the financial area of your chart today; therefore any extravagance should be avoided at all costs over the ensuing weeks. Opt for cheaper entertainment.

29th – It is important that you keep a close watch on your moveable property during the next few weeks. Hang on to your purse and wallet when in crowds, especially during the next couple of days.

30th – Financial rewards will come to those expecting bonus payments or extra money for work done in the past. Gamblers should also have a lucky day. Avoid all kinds of 'under-the-counter' deals.

31st – The month goes out on a confused note. Partners and loved ones are diffident and difficult to understand; their behaviour will be erratic and very trying. Keep calm and handle them with care.

April

1st – Romance looks promising, especially if you are looking for Mr/Miss Right. You will not have to go searching for it, it will come to you. A good day for all personal relationships. Work is mundane.

2nd – Anyone who has finances at risk will see a satisfactory outcome today. For people involved in litigation, you will also be on the winning side. Comforting news.

3rd – All appears to be quiet on the marriage front, although partners may still be behaving in a rather haphazard manner. Try to find out exactly what is on their minds before letting off steam.

4th – This is the middle of the New Moon period and it makes an excellent time for travelling, sorting out the problems of brothers and sisters, and on a professional basis publicizing your talents as much as possible. Not a time to be the shrinking violet, then.

5th – Minor accidents are predicted at home, and this also applies to children in and around the house. Today is a time when you could quite easily be taken for a ride financially, so avoid the shops.

6th – Those in work which could be described as behind the scenes will find today both profitable and enjoyable. Great strides can be taken. Aquarians at home will have many interruptions to contend with.

7th – Do not put pleasure before duty, as there are routine matters which need clearing up before you can begin to enjoy yourself. Make plans for spending a special weekend with a loved one.

8th – Those away from home will find that today runs exactly as yesterday. If you are at home you could find that an older relative makes a flying visit which is disruptive and unenjoyable.

9th – Rely on your logical side when taking financial decisions; flights of fantasy will only get you into deep water. Those with joint finances at risk should handle them very carefully.

10th – A favourable day for trying out new and revolutionary ideas. There are ways of making extra cash which only now reveal themselves. It is a time when all good ideas can be put into practice.

11th – No point in trying to impress relatives or friends, your powers of persuasion are nil. If attending get-togethers with them, let other and more sparkling personalities do most of the talking for the time being. Romance bites the dust.

12th – Not a good day for family discussions; you will find members of your household reluctant to sit down for longer than five minutes. Ideally it is a time to spend travelling around visiting friends, neighbours and relatives.

13th – You will be bored with routine and in a restless mood. Try to keep your interest centred on the job in hand, otherwise you will make mistakes that will be costly in terms of both time and money.

14th – Do not take exception if those around you are receiving more attention than your good self. Your time will come later. If attending to work around the home, be careful to avoid accidents.

15th – Not a good day for planning home improvements, or for making career decisions, as your judgement is unreliable. Allow other people to dictate the day's events.

16th – Those having to travel in the course of their work find that short journeys are fraught with delay. If possible, put off business meetings until a better time.

17th – This is the day of the Full Moon and it falls in the working and career part of your solar chart. Take care therefore to avoid new projects, but finish off existing jobs and keep a low profile. Changes are taking place and you don't want one of them to be you!

18th – Not a favourable day for those hoping to get together with new acquaintances or lovers; it is likely that you will be stood up. It might be a good idea to double-check your diary and make a few calls before leaving home.

19th – You will not be in the best of moods early in the day, and this could lead to conflict with the family. However, this afternoon you should be back to your usual sunny self and the day will end on a happy note.

20th – Not a day for giving advice to others, especially where it has not been asked for. People will accuse you of interfering in things that don't concern you. What is more – they will be right.

21st – Get out and about today, and leave routine matters of the home to look after themselves. This afternoon is a good time for the gambler, as Lady Luck is perched on your shoulder.

22nd – The Sun moves into Taurus today, so during the next few weeks the emphasis will be on family, property and domestic matters in general. Important decisions will be needed in these areas.

23rd – A good day for making long-distance visits to relatives or friends. Travel is well-aspected and journeys should go without a hitch. Try to relax this evening before retiring for the night.

24th – All financial affairs should have a satisfactory outcome, especially if you have been hinting at a rise in salary for some time. Those at home should receive some good news in the mail.

25th – If you have had health problems for some while, now is the time to do something about them. This is a good day for attending to all matters concerning your personal well-being.

26th – Romance could rear its head in connection with friends or acquaintances, but those who are married should guard against straying from the straight and narrow path. Get younger people to participate in the evening's entertainment.

27th – The personal side of your life will take precedence, as your career appears to be managing itself. Some new and exciting invitations should come your way this afternoon. A fresh circle of friends is in the offing.

28th – There appears to be a pleasant surprise in store, due to the intervention of a friend into your plans. Financial considerations are paramount when planning a holiday.

29th – Get away from the home base today, as there is a sentimental side to your nature which needs catering to. Visit places that bring back happy memories and enjoy the company of very old friends.

30th – You are likely to join forces with other people today in an effort to boost your finances. This is not such a bad idea, as partnership affairs are well-aspected.

May

1st – You are sure to feel left out of things, but don't worry as this will work to your advantage. Take a back seat when attending business discussions. Financial success is indicated this afternoon.

2nd – This is the day of the New Moon and it falls in the domestic, family and property area of your chart. There is bound to be a minor new cycle in connection with these affairs in the very near future. A great day for house-hunting.

3rd – Romantic chances are good today, especially for those looking for Mr or Miss Right. Those people who are working behind the scenes are sure to be rewarded for their past efforts in the near future. Plan a personal celebration this evening.

4th – Do not try to handle anything that is experimental or adventurous, as you will not be able to complete it. Stick to routine matters, both in your domestic environment and at work.

5th – Not a good day for those redecorating or refurbishing the home. Jobs of this kind which are tackled will not have the expected results. This evening will see you depressed, and in the company of friends.

6th – A bad day for contacting those at a distance; the news you hear will not put you in a good mood. This afternoon should be spent laying down plans for a long trip or holiday.

7th – Your plans are likely to fall through today, when people on whom you are dependent for support now let you down. A source of income is suddenly cut off.

8th – Do not gossip, either at work or over the garden wall. You will be accused later on of being the instigator. Younger people will come to you for financial advice this afternoon – do not give any, as you may lead them astray.

9th – The Moon is in your opposition today, so take your cues from those around you rather than pushing ahead on your own. You are lacking in judgement. Imagination also seems to have run dry, so hand over the social arrangements to those closest to you.

10th – The unattainable will attract you today, and this could be either a much-longed-for possession or a person. Friends are full of bounce this evening and this exhausts you; plan an early night if at all possible.

11th – Those working in areas of research should have an inspired day. All good ideas which occur to you now should be put into operation immediately. Financial discussions with a partner get under way.

12th – Do not raise the hopes of a work colleague who comes to you with a problem. Your counsel should be blunt and to the point. Count your own blessings and not those of someone else.

13th – An excellent day for getting what you want from other people without trying too hard. Favours granted now will benefit you in the near future.

14th – Do not over-react to the criticism of others; they are only trying to point you in the right direction. You don't always know best. Children will be very demanding this evening.

15th – Do not chop and change plans which have already been made, but stick to your guns and follow your chosen course. Financially, this is a good afternoon when gains can be made.

16th – This is the day of the Full Moon, and it falls in the zenith of your chart. Time, then, to finish off work which has been hanging fire for some considerable time; leave new projects to a later date. When socializing, stick to the tried and true. Experiments will not work.

17th – Keep all you are doing today on very simple lines, stick to routine and don't attempt anything out of the ordinary. Relatives and loved ones who have been supporting you will now make good their promises.

18th – Tie up all loose ends with your work and start to lay down plans for a short break. Work colleagues will probably be offering invitations that you should accept – you can glean some vital information in this way.

19th – A good day for all of this sign who are in organizational occupations. Sporting fixtures go without a hitch. Gamblers are advised to keep their stakes to a minimum. Romance is unsettled for the single.

20th – Older people will feature in the day's activities. Hospitals are in evidence, so perhaps you will visit a relative who is confined there at present. This evening will be hectic, but enjoyable.

21st – Start the day as you mean to carry on. You can make good progress now provided you show a confident façade. Do not allow superiors to overload you with work.

22nd – Those around you could be getting themselves into a bit of a muddle, and it is up to you to sort them out. Do so willingly, as you will need a favour or two later in the year.

23rd – A plan or social arrangement which you were confidently expecting to materialize will fall through, leaving you feeling somewhat disillusioned and disappointed. Make up for it by having a good time this evening.

24th – You are self-reliant and discriminating. Choose your emotional partners carefully. A younger member of the opposite sex will give you some interesting information – act upon it.

25th – Take a back seat today and allow the mainstream of events to take place around you. There is no point in trying to get your views across, as you will be blocked at every twist and turn.

26th – Check and double-check all that you attempt, as mistakes are likely to be made. There is also a danger of loss through theft, so make certain that your personal possessions are under lock and key.

27th – The romantic side to your nature should be kept very strictly under control when dealing with members of the opposite sex on a business level. You could ruin something very promising by being too forward today.

28th – Early-morning blues could make it difficult for you to get along with colleagues; bite your lip when you feel a tantrum coming on. Domestic affairs take a turn for the better.

29th – Minor health problems associated with headaches and dental problems could ruin a day full of possibilities. Try to fight your way through, as good opportunities abound. Relax in the company of friends this evening, but seek medical attention soon.

30th – The wrong time to get anything new under way. Stick to routine affairs. Financial losses are indicated as a result of hasty decisions. Allow partners to make all financial arrangements just now.

31st – Make certain that all loose ends are tied when leaving work tonight, as they will be hard to pick up in the morning. Friends could be a source of irritation this evening. Stick with your loved ones.

June

1st – This is New Moon day and it falls in Gemini, the fun area of your chart which is related to speculation, entertainment, socializing and romance. New beginnings are expected in these directions and romance is well-starred too.

2nd – If you are an artist or in a creative profession you will be receiving an interesting proposition. Think it through carefully and seek professional advice if you think this is necessary.

3rd – Do not waste too much time discussing future career plans, as they will have to be changed at the last minute. Travel is not well-aspected, and you would do better if you let others make the arrangements.

4th – This is ideally a day of pleasure, but unfortunately you will not be feeling up to enjoying yourself. Stick your nose to the grindstone and slog away. Careful thought will be needed regarding the evening's entertainment.

5th – Romance is likely for the single, and married Aquarians will reach a deeper understanding. Very personal family affairs should be attended to now; there is a likelihood of an early engagement.

6th – Minor health problems will rear their heads, brought about by periods of inactivity. Those dieting at present will find it difficult to get rid of that unwanted fat, but don't lose heart.

7th – All financial transactions carried out on behalf of a third party stand an excellent chance of success, especially as it is likely that friends are involved. Socially, you prefer to stay at home and read a good book, but this may bring a few cross words from loved ones. You may have to force yourself out and about.

8th – Financial rewards will be coming through the post this morning, so you are advised to check it out thoroughly. Late this afternoon you will receive a telephone call which could change your way of seeing things.

9th – Plan your day's activities well as they are likely to go off the rails, disappointing many. Loved ones will be looking to you to provide an alternative. The financial outlay is greater than usual.

10th – This should be a hectic day, with friends and relatives popping in and out all of the time. This evening is the best period for arranging entertainment. Expenses will be sky-rocketing where children are concerned.

11th – You could suffer from lapses of memory, leading to mistakes. Care should be taken in this direction, as time and money will be wasted. Telephone calls will be important to you this evening.

12th – Career matters take a back seat today as there appears to be a domestic problem for you to sort out. The advice of an elderly relative should be heeded. Parents will find children a source of irritation.

13th – The Moon in Sagittarius suggests that this is an excellent time for visiting a club or getting together with old friends. It is likely that you will be meeting new acquaintances in this way, and indirectly a romance could blossom for the singles.

14th – In-laws are trying to make their presence felt at this particular moment in time; their interference in a domestic problem could lead to it being prolonged. Advice is best taken from friends.

15th – Show other people that you mean business today. A forceful approach will work wonders for you and your career. Romance is likely to occur where an introduction is made by friends.

16th – Deception is the ruling factor today, and housewives will be particularly vulnerable in this respect. Those involved in the arts are prone to self-deception.

17th – Get away from it all today if possible, and set aside some periods for rest and relaxation. Friends should be given short shrift if they try to interrupt your solitude. This evening will be romantic for the married Aquarian.

18th – Work colleagues will tax your patience today and you will need plenty of tact in order to avoid a confrontation. Financial aspects are good, and you are likely to make a few small gains.

19th – Aquarians thinking of making changes in their career or domestic lives should hold back until the aspects are more favourable. Those who are beginning new jobs today will have no difficulties to overcome.

20th – The Moon is in your sign this Saturday, therefore it should be relatively easy for you to get your own way. Further, you are more flexible and sensitive than is usually the case, and this will delight your loved ones.

21st – It appears that you are spending too much time worrying. Try to sort out your mental condition and turn your energy to practical use. Children will give parents a hard time today.

22nd – You will take a long time to get to grips with a job in hand, and this could lead to frustration in those around you. Make definite plans on how to best use your talent and time.

23rd – A good time for setting off on long-distance journeys. If your work takes you far from home you will have a good day, as will those about to set off on holiday. Those at home should give some time to meeting the demands of relatives.

24th – A romantic atmosphere should pervade the homes of all married couples. The single will find it difficult to understand a new romantic partner, and their behaviour could leave a lot to be desired.

25th – Whatever you plan for the early part of the day will run smoothly, but you could find yourself being blocked this afternoon. Therefore attend to all important items this morning.

26th – Impulsive behaviour could land you in trouble with a superior or an old and valued friend. Try to keep these tendencies under control. Loved ones will be cooperative and understanding; makes plans for the future.

27th – Changes going on around you will eventually work to your advantage if you have the staying power. Do not allow older relatives to throw you off balance. Younger people appear to be more to your liking today.

28th – Avoid DIY jobs as mistakes are likely this morning which will lead to your having to do extra work at a later date. If routine chores are hard for you to take, why not get together with friends even if it's only for a pub lunch?

29th – Financially this is one of your better days. Gains will be made in all areas. Those connected with research could find themselves up for an award of some description.

30th – The month goes out on a financial high note. Gamblers should not be afraid to put cash at risk, while housewives will find bargains easily in their own locale. A good day for handling the problems of offspring.

July

1st – Adopt a competitive attitude and do not allow others to push you into something which you really don't wish to do. You have a variety of options open to you where entertainment is concerned this evening.

2nd – Let those around you set the pace while you follow along in their footsteps. There is little point in pushing yourself to the fore. This evening is a good time for home entertaining.

3rd – A day when your nerves could let you down, therefore you are advised to tackle only those jobs with which you are familiar. Tasks which require a great deal of concentration and effort should be left to hang fire.

4th – Those around you will be doing more for you today than you are doing for yourself. Allow this state of affairs to continue for a while. Your judgement is faulty, so it is not a time for making decisions.

5th – If you are hunting for a new house you could strike lucky this afternoon. This morning should be used for catching up with personal correspondence and contacting those who live or work at a distance. Visit neighbours this evening.

6th – People in business partnerships should let their opposite number take all the decisions. If you are quite happy to take a back seat, these important issues will take care of themselves.

7th – This is a good time to make a fresh start on new jobs around the home, but make certain that previous tasks have had their ends securely tied. Relatives could make life difficult this evening if you do not give in to their demands.

8th – Do try to spend the day as quietly as possible. Callers who arrive unannounced should be sent packing. You may hurt a number of feelings but the effect will not be long-lasting. Plan an early night too.

9th – Those whose jobs could be described as being behind the scenes will know today whether or not promotion is theirs. If you have been angling for this, you can expect some good news.

10th – A financially favourable day for all those connected with the medical profession. Others should find that the morning post contains some good news and also something unexpected.

11th – A good day for bringing yourself to the attention of members of the opposite sex whom you've had your eye on for some considerable time. Routine matters within the home can be speeded up with the application of a little forethought and planning.

12th – If you are creative or scientific you can make good use of this Sunday. Clear a backlog of routine matters and set your mind thinking about a new challenge for the week ahead. Others will find this a rather dull day.

13th – Something you lost some while ago should make an appearance this morning. This is a day for unexpected events, most of which will work to your advantage. Let others take the lead this evening.

14th – This is the day of the Full Moon and it may find you in a tetchy, insecure and rather strange mood. Don't worry about this phase, it will soon pass – and in the meantime avoid taking yourself or other people too seriously.

15th – Venus is now firmly in your opposition, throwing a golden glow over all existing relationships. Now is a wonderful time for arranging engagements or marriages. If you are single, you will meet someone of real value at this stage.

16th – Do not waste the day attending to trivial matters, but get on with something that you consider important. You could be accused of time-wasting by your colleagues; put them right in no uncertain terms.

17th – A minor health problem could ruin your day if you do not get it attended to. Headaches and eyestrain are your worst enemies. This afternoon will see good opportunities coming your way.

18th – All appears to be going well on the marriage front; also, the single could find the person of their dreams. Care should be taken, however, if you are married and wish to stray from the straight and narrow path.

19th – Your supply of energy could let you down today, and you may have to call upon a friend to complete a task on your behalf. This evening is a time for family celebrations and home entertaining.

20th – Your generosity could get the better of you, and extravagance will be the result. You love to give, but should do so only with reservations. This afternoon will find you calling on those who live at a distance.

21st – Let the day's events go on around you, as you will not feel up to taking part in the activities. Friends will come to your aid this evening when you find yourself at a loose end.

22nd – Romance is in the air. The single will find a casual affair developing into something more substantial, and the marrieds should find that partners reveal a deeper side to their characters.

23rd – Keep all your plans to modest proportions, especially if you work in any kind of research. Overstepping the mark could damage your chances of promotion. Progress will be made financially by all.

24th – The Sun is now in your opposition, therefore the success of the next few weeks will depend on your ability to give support and to cooperate. Forget about going off at a tangent.

25th – This morning will be a very slow-moving time and your greatest enemy will be boredom. Try to find something new to attempt. Routine work within the home will take on a different character today.

26th – Be cautious when entering into joint financial commitments. You will need to understand exactly what is required of you before planning any legal documents during the week. A reunion looks likely this evening.

27th – Where other people are concerned, you could be accused of raising false hopes. Keep your information to yourself. This afternoon is the best time for making contact with people who have been elusive.

28th – Begin the day as you mean to carry on, especially if you have brought work home to complete it. Loved ones could complain of neglect, but you will be able to put that to rights this evening.

29th – This is a day of the New Moon and it falls in your opposition, suggesting a fresh set of circumstances in one of your relationships and the possibility of a new romance for the single.

30th – Beware of over-estimating your worth and your capabilities as you are likely to bite off more than you can comfortably chew. If you are thinking of making either a domestic or a career change, in a word – don't!

31st Give way to the wishes of others today, despite having every intention of blocking the plans of someone else. This afternoon will see minor health problems subsiding. Entertain at home this evening.

August

1st – You have a tense and nervous day, being irritable with those around you. Try to remain calm in the face of adversity. This evening is a bad time for family get-togethers; stick to friends instead.

2nd – A good day for married couples to get out and about and enjoy themselves whenever possible. Those on holiday will have an exceptionally enjoyable time. Care should be taken while travelling.

3rd – Romance can be found at your place of work. Someone there is paying you a lot of attention with this very thought in mind. Financial matters receive a boost this evening.

4th – Do not allow people to upset you today. You will be ready to fly off the handle at the slightest excuse or pretext. Superiors are unhelpful in the realization of a new project or idea.

5th – Those involved in the financial professions should have an exciting and profitable day. Others will find that finances are boosted and bonus payments will be above average. This evening is good for home entertaining.

6th – Relatives will upset your arrangements for the coming weekend by changing direction at the last minute. Go ahead with your plans regardless, however, and do not give in to social or emotional blackmail.

7th – Rushing about will achieve nothing today; everything you do should be carried out quite methodically. This afternoon is a good time for visiting relatives you have not seen for some while.

8th – Minor health problems could be sapping your energy. If there is anything untoward in this respect, have it sorted out as soon as possible. Social arrangements will offer plenty of opportunities for meeting interesting new members of the opposite sex.

9th – Financial losses are indicated today through carelessness – better hang on to your cash and personal possessions. If travelling, make certain that you have double-checked all of your arrangements.

10th – A new relationship begun today will have you planning ahead. Do not bother, however, since what appears to be permanent is unstable. This afternoon a work colleague will show his true colours.

11th – Take your time where routine work is concerned – mistakes can be easily made in this area. Carefully apply yourself to all work in hand and refrain from making unnecessary changes.

12th – Do not be too eager to change boats in mid-stream; finish off one job before starting on another. Work colleagues will be uncooperative and downright obstructive. Attempt to proceed around them.

13th – Get yourself involved in the plans of others, since this is not a day on which to make your own entertainment. The financial outlay could be very heavy this evening.

14th – This is the day of the Full Moon, so make no attempt to start anything fresh – whether it be relationships, projects or work. Take particular care of possessions, as some of them could go walkabout.

15th – It is likely that a contract may have run its course. If so, make some plans this Saturday to find fresh outlets for your talents. Make sure that you do some relaxing and get out and have fun this evening.

16th – A relative will have some bearing on the day's events. It appears that a family problem needs a solution, and quickly. Consultations with friends could provide you with an answer.

17th – You have a clear way in front of you today, so it should be full steam ahead. Do not be backward in coming forward; go all out for whatever you desire in any area of your life.

18th – There is an opportunity for career advancement today, but only if you take the bull by the horns. Other people will not put things on a plate for you, so create your own opportunities.

19th – Romance looks set for ripening, but you should not put too much faith in your present partner. Your judgement will be seriously lacking, therefore make no long-term commitments.

20th – Those returning from holiday will be feeling very down in the dumps; a bout of depression will spoil your day. Try to occupy your mind as much as possible and refrain from being idle.

21st – Not a good day for travelling, so you are advised to stay close to your home base. Entertaining friends and relatives in your own home will be especially enjoyable.

22nd – This is an especially good day for getting into the great outdoors. An interesting new acquaintance may make a financial offer which appears to relieve you of financial pressure for the time being, but you should consider this well before making commitments.

23rd – Too many people are involved in an idea of yours, and you will be feeling pushed into the background and somewhat disgruntled. Make your feelings known to all and sundry. Step up and seize the limelight this evening.

24th – Another accident-prone day, when you should avoid all contact with hot and sharp objects. Those operating complicated heavy machinery are also advised to take extra care.

25th – Romance in the lives of the married will add a greater depth to the relationship. A day when someone may be holding out the hand of friendship which you are inadvertently ignoring.

26th – If you are travelling today, you will find the attentions of a stranger interesting and exciting, but do not take anything they say or promise too seriously.

27th – Social butterflies will gain most from today, as this is a time for party-going and general celebrations. However, others should watch their expenditure as money will be wasted hand over fist.

28th – A telephone call could bring you into contact with someone you have not seen for quite a while, perhaps an old flame or school chum. This evening is a great time for catching up with correspondence and general paperwork.

29th – This is the middle of the New Moon period and it's definitely a case 'off with the old and on with the new.' Put the past firmly behind you and look to the future, especially during the next six months which could be vitally important.

30th – Headaches and minor health problems beset you and you will certainly be feeling below par. Relatives will come to your aid, but you will be loath to allow them to complete any job on which you have set your heart.

31st – A happier day, especially for the marrieds, although the single will still be chasing rainbows and getting nowhere. Work problems upset you this afternoon, and you will end the day in an irritable frame of mind.

September

1st – Those connected with sports in any capacity will have a difficult day. Confine yourself to more sedentary occupations. Work around the home will be subject to interruption and delay.

2nd – Not the best day to make courtesy calls, be they personal or professional – especially to older relatives, whose behaviour will be erratic and, in some cases, eccentric. Younger people may provide better entertainment and interest.

3rd – Social invitations extended to you by work colleagues should be accepted, as you will learn something to your advantage. This afternoon should be used for catching up on neglected routine work.

4th – A day of muddle and misunderstanding, therefore you should postpone making any decisions of importance until later. Allow other people to take the reins while you sit back and enjoy the ride.

5th – Your judgement is faulty, and you could do someone a great disservice by making snap decisions as to their character. Be sure you have all the facts right before indulging in gossip.

6th – This is a day you will be happy to play the recluse. Your partner may be dismayed by your anti-social behaviour, so try to explain the reason and this should lead to a peaceful day. Arrangements may have to be cancelled.

7th – You could be in danger of wasting too much time. Make decisions and stick to them instead of considering all the pros and cons at length. Colleagues will be getting impatient with your procrastination.

8th – Entertainment plans will go awry due to your indecision, so allow friends or relatives to make the arrangements. If travelling, make certain you are sure of your route before setting out.

9th – Begin the day as you mean to go on. You are mentally and physically at your best and should be able to make valuable progress. Superiors are attracted to you and your ideas, so make the most of this.

10th – Do not spend too much time in the realms of fantasy today; try to keep in touch with the realities of what is happening around you. A period of reflection is likely this evening.

11th – Practical matters take on a new light, through either the acquisition of cash or the loss of it. Financial offers will not be all they seem, and you should look deeply into any suggestions that are made in this area.

12th – The Full Moon in Pisces suggests that you hang on to possessions like grim death. Also, it is possible that over the next few days there could be a loss of a source of income, and you may have to find a replacement urgently. Avoid the shops and any unnecessary cash outlay.

13th – Romance is in the air, although you should not attach too much importance to it. Relationships begun today will not have a lasting quality. Those who are married will find their partners difficult to understand.

14th – Social invitations which come your way should be accepted, especially if they afford you the opportunity of meeting new friends. Housewives should shop in their normal neighbourhoods where bargains are easier to come by.

15th – Work done at home today could cause you to neglect your partner or loved one. Set aside a period for relaxation for yourself and allow some time for their problems. Entertainment comes through friends.

16th – A fairly quiet day, when all you have to attend to will be the problems of younger members of the family. Relatives are easygoing and surprise visits by them are appreciated this evening.

17th – A good day for clearing away all inessentials from your life. Career progress will be hindered by jealous work colleagues; it is about time you educated them as to your ambitions.

18th – Those attending interviews should push themselves to the fore. Also, the unemployed could strike lucky by being more forceful. Partnership affairs are likely to suffer from indecision.

19th – Friends or work colleagues who try to involve you in get-rich-quick schemes should be given a wide birth. They are up to something that is not quite legal. Do not invest cash in any suspect projects.

20th – Make sure you are aware of what is going on around you. Things are changing in the family, and you should take advantage of this. This evening is the best time for entertaining 'that special someone' at your home.

21st – Financial gains are indicated today. Windfalls are likely and there is also the possibility of cash coming through official channels. Friends make ideal companions this evening, but are likely to be expensive.

22nd – Set your targets today and do not give up until you achieve them, otherwise you are likely to waste your time and energy on useless projects. If visiting, make certain that people know you are coming.

23rd – A hectic time, with much to-ing and fro-ing as unexpected guests and visitors abound. You are likely to end the day with the house full. Someone who comes to stay for a short time will stay around for what seems to be for ever!

24th – Do not put your faith in anyone who makes promises of long-term support, financial or otherwise. Career progress can be made by your own efforts. A day of self-reliance.

25th – You will have to be quick to follow up career leads if

you are to take advantage of prevailing conditions. Financially, this is a day of minor gains and losses. Do not be too optimistic.
26th – You begin to realize that a new plan or project is hopelessly lost. Do not waste valuable time trying to pick up the pieces, but get busy on the next one.
27th – This a New Moon period and you are starting to feel more able to cope with all your problems. Extra responsibility which has recently fallen on your shoulders begins to carry with it the promise of promotion. This afternoon is a good time for making long-distance calls or visiting relatives.
28th – Do not allow slower people to dictate the pace today. Keep your nose down and much will be achieved. It appears that a member of the opposite sex will be important in the day's events.
29th – If travelling long distances today, make certain that your method of transport is reliable. Delays and disappointments will be caused by breakdowns. Stay at home and you will end the day frustrated and bored, however.
30th – Use the quiet of today to catch up on a backlog of personal correspondence and suchlike. A period of self-improvement will appeal, but you will not have the tenacity to keep it up for very long.

October

1st – If travelling today make certain that you are wrapped up against the elements, as colds and chills are likely to be contracted while on the move. Financial gains are likely for those willing to take a chance.
2nd – Those connected with buying and selling, export/import and family businesses should have a profitable day. Financial matters come under review, and you could be pleasantly surprised at the outcome.
3rd – Romance is likely for the single; a partner may be found at your place of work. Expect the unexpected where your career is concerned and be ready to take advantage of all opportunities.
4th – Do not be tempted to go back into the past today. Spending too much time on past mistakes or reminiscences will lead you nowhere. Friends are easily contacted this afternoon and will be willing to discuss your future with you.
5th – A good day for Aquarians who are travelling in the course of their business. New contacts will be made and lucrative con-

tracts will be offered. Others should view all financial offers with suspicion.

6th – A favourable time for those connected with sports in any form; participants will taste success and organizers should see profits. This evening is a good time for gathering the family around you.

7th – Friends take up the better part of the day; their company will be stimulating and their ideas interesting. This evening is the best time for spending with a loved one or relative.

8th – Younger people have a great say in the day's events, and you should be prepared to listen to what they have to tell. You are likely to be over-critical with loved ones this evening, which will cause conflict.

9th – Do not allow colleagues to dictate the pace, but work at your own rate. Challenging jobs which come your way this afternoon will provide a pleasing break from routine – which incidentally should not be neglected.

10th – Minor health problems – perhaps associated with over-work or sporting activities – will dog your footsteps today. Set aside time for rest and relaxation. Finances improve this afternoon with an unexpected windfall or gift.

11th – All forms of communication are important at present, and you should not neglect telephone calls or messages. This evening is a good time for beginning a new course of self-improvement. Foreign languages may appeal.

12th – Friends and colleagues may let you down at the last minute, and a new joint project will have to be shelved. Relatives are cantankerous and difficult to please this evening, and you will end the day irritable.

13th – Get out and about today, but be careful when travelling under your own steam. Transport problems will cause disappointment, so it would be best to stick to public transport. Old friends contact you this evening.

14th – An old flame is about to put in an appearance, so reassure present partners that the embers can never be rekindled. Parents will find it difficult to come to terms with the problems of offspring.

15th – A good day for contacting superiors with career problems. Colleagues are obstructive this afternoon and you are advised to go it alone. This is not a favourable time for financial matters; losses are indicated.

16th – Minor health problems should have subsided and you will have more energy to cope with things that you consider important. Routine matters which have been neglected cause some trouble later in the day.

17th – You may find it necessary to take work home this evening; if this is the case, you will need the cooperation of partners. Make certain that you do nothing to antagonize them in any way.

18th – Romance for the single is likely; also, marriage partners are at their most romantic. Cooperation from relatives will make your day a pleasant one, and they may even have interesting ideas on your ambitions.

19th – Do not give way over a point of principle as your judgement is on the ball now. Beware of taking strangers into your confidence, as you will give away far more than you learn.

20th – Not the best day of the week for attempting work in or around the home; minor accidents are likely. If working in high, exposed places, make certain that all safety precautions are observed. Financial good luck is indicated this evening.

21st – If you feel you have been over-critical with a loved one, now is the time to make your apologies. Relatives are not in the best of moods, so it would be best to stay away from them. Friends make good companions.

22nd – Give work colleagues all the help you can, and they will return the favour when you need it most. It is a good time for pushing ahead with your career, and for reaching an understanding with an older person.

23rd – The Sun has entered Scorpio and you begin the most ambitious part of the year. Be sure, though, that you do not neglect loved ones or they will complain loudly over the ensuing weeks. Progress should be spectacular.

24th – Expect the unexpected in all areas of life today. Let nothing throw you off the rails. Those who are married should not take the flirtatious behaviour of their partners too seriously; certainly don't make a fuss unnecessarily.

25th – This is the day of the New Moon; it is difficult to imagine you being able to completely relax, for work colleagues are sure to be on the phone with some exciting news. You can expect changes and new beginnings where career matters are concerned.

26th – Keep everything moving steadily forward today; if you allow yourself to be side-tracked, progress will be impossible.

Housewives should steer clear of doorstep salesmen, since bargains will not be up to expectations.

27th – Shopping sprees are inadvisable today; too much money will be spent on non-essentials. Most entertainment comes expensive today, so you would be advised to keep things along simple lines.

28th – Friends have financial offers to make, but you should have nothing to do with them. Hare-brained schemes will not work out to your advantage. This evening is a good time for paying courtesy calls on relatives.

29th – Minor health problems will have eased and marriage disagreements have now been sorted out. Now you can get into top gear and stay there for a while. Push ahead with your cherished hopes and wishes.

30th – Financial offers which come your way should be sound, but better be safe than sorry. Anything you do not understand should be explained fully to you. This afternoon is a good time for gamblers.

31st – Romance is in for some trouble, though only of a minor nature. Provided you are sensible and willing to see the other side of the argument, no harm should come to your steady or permanent relationship.

November

1st – A better financial outlook is on the way, and it should begin with a surprise windfall or present today. Everyone should benefit to some extent from the prevailing conditions.

2nd – Mistakes made this morning will be extremely difficult to rectify at a later date, therefore leave DIY jobs well alone. The Moon is in your sign at present. Time to occupy centre stage now – the opposite sex will find you positively irresistible.

3rd – Not a good day for putting finances at risk. Gamblers should keep stakes to a minimum, as more will be lost than won. This evening will see your outgoings rising on expensive entertainment.

4th – Try to plan a quiet day away from spendthrift friends. Those with more cash than yourself will expect you to keep up with them. Don't even try – explain your position instead.

5th – Nerves are likely to be your greatest enemy this week, coupled with a feeling of lethargy. It would be best to steer clear of all strenuous physical tasks. Try to confine yourself to intellectual pursuits over the next couple of days.

6th – A very romantic time is forecast for the marrieds; partners are cooperative and willing to please. However, the single will experience difficulties with new relationships. Financial gains are likely this evening.

7th – Personal possessions will have a habit of disappearing just when you need them, so keep your eye on them. Motorists are advised to be on their guard when driving, as minor brushes with the law are likely.

8th – Those connected with publishing and buying and selling have a good period coming up; plan ahead now in order to get the most from it. Others will find that short-term plans put into operation now will be successful.

9th – Check and double-check all work you do today – silly mistakes are likely to be overlooked. Financial problems seem to be easing, but you will still need to be thrifty for a while longer.

10th – This is the day of the Full Moon and it's not a good time for gadding about – especially if you are considering house-hunting. If you have to venture forth make certain that you are well protected, as chills will be contracted while out and about.

11th – A hectic day with much coming and going at your home. Friends will be popping in and bringing new colleagues with them. You are about to enter a new circle of friends, a club or association.

12th – You continue to make mistakes at work, and these will cost you dear unless you rectify them before leaving for the day. Many of you will be taking work home. Younger people are fun to be with this evening.

13th – Care should be taken when dealing with superiors as you are likely to fly off the handle, giving a totally wrong picture of yourself. Use a little charm – it will go a long, long way.

14th – A good Saturday for handling all matters that you consider of importance to yourself. Forget what other people think. Emotional and romantic problems can be smoothed out with relative ease; just use a certain amount of charm and affection.

15th – Clear the dead wood from your life. Old opinions and outdated thinking should be cast aside, otherwise you will not make headway. Changes that you make during the next few days will benefit you in the future.

16th – Romance is definitely in the air, especially for the single, but this is not a time to attach too much credence to it. Go ahead and enjoy yourself. Married Aquarians will find partners very loving and affectionate.

17th – It appears that you will be taking care of things for a relative who will possibly be hospitalized for a short period. Be as helpful as you can and give your time freely.

18th – Try to make friends understand that you would like to spend today on your own. You will need tact and diplomacy, but that should be in good supply. Plan an early night.

19th – Minor health problems should begin to ease and you will feel more like your old self. Energy could be low, however, so you are advised not to tackle anything too strenuous.

20th – Finances take a turn for the better and an unexpected windfall comes your way. This afternoon is the best time for dealing with all money matters. Career problems should be discussed with superiors.

21st – You will probably be shouldering extra responsibilities today, on both a business and a personal level. Romantic relationships are deepening and many will be thinking of making a long-term commitment.

22nd – This may be a Sunday, but it will be hard to turn your mind from work and an associate will probably be getting in touch. Those involved in a partnership will soon be picking up greater profits. If you are trying to get jobs done around the home you will have to contend with interruptions and delays.

23rd – Not the best day of the month for going it alone. Enlist the help of colleagues wherever possible. This evening is best spent in the company of friends who amuse and stimulate you.

24th – This is the day of the New Moon and it falls in the friendship area of your chart, suggesting that you will be meeting a fresh set of friends. Make sure you don't spend money in an effort to keep up with them.

25th – Courtesy calls to business contacts or elderly relatives should be enjoyable and satisfying to all parties. You are at your best at present, and your company will be greatly appreciated by all.

26th – The day gets off to a good start and you are full of energy. Proceed with confidence whatever your aim. Long-term plans can be put into operation and favours can be asked from superiors and colleagues alike.

27th – Further changes at your place of work will be to your advantage, especially if your business is connected with publishing or the literary world. This evening is a good time for catching up on neglected correspondence.

28th – Older work colleagues will come to your aid with their experience and expertise. Do not be too proud to take the hand held out to you. Financial gains can be made this afternoon.

29th – All should be bliss on the marriage front, and single people will be turning their thoughts towards marriage. Finances settle down and you will find opportunities arising to make some extra money.

30th – The month goes out on a romantic note. Married Aquarians are feeling a deeper understanding with their partners. The unattached single should look for love amongst those introduced to them by friends.

December

1st – Give older people the benefit of the doubt, even if it goes against the grain. Housewives should get out and look for good bargains, which can be found in the most unexpected places today.

2nd – Not a day for sitting around letting the grass grow; get out and about and search for some adventure. It is a fine day for attempting things you have not experienced before. A little experimental work will help with relationships.

3rd – There are people around you at present who are trying to obstruct your career ambitions, and they will need to be told off in no uncertain terms. This afternoon is good for all long-distance communications.

4th – You are very magnetic today and find that people are attracted to you and your talents. Therefore now is an excellent time for putting yourself on display to superiors. New projects begun at this time are sure to be successful. Take full advantage of the aspects.

5th – Romance is likely for the single, and a relationship begun now will last for a long time. Those who are single and already in permanent relationships will be making important and serious commitments.

6th – A favourable day from the financial viewpoint. Gains will be made through your own efforts, perhaps from a small gamble. This afternoon is good for entertaining relatives or friends you have not seen for some time.

7th – Personal possessions should be watched all the time today as they are likely to disappear, either through theft or through being mislaid. This is not a good day for putting your money at risk, especially if you are thinking of becoming involved with a friend.

8th – Let other people arrange the entertainment today. You need a rest from organization. Friends will be keen to provide a diversion, but their ideas may be too expensive for your taste.

9th – This is the day of the Full Moon and it falls in Gemini, therefore it is likely that a social occasion may be cancelled or a romance may come to a grinding halt. Keep an extra eye on children; they may be off-colour or slightly accident-prone.

10th – Those around you are in a mood for some fun and you will not think twice before joining in. Care should be taken, however, as you are in danger of developing minor health disorders.

11th – Try to obtain the approval of superiors before putting ideas into operation. You could be guilty of stepping on someone's toes or of undermining their authority.

12th – A good day for long-distance travel. Your arrangements will be foolproof and your journey enjoyable. Not so for those to-ing and fro-ing around the local neighbourhood, however – many delays are likely.

13th – Headaches and tiredness will be your main enemies today, therefore you are advised not to attempt any jobs that require concentration or attention to detail. Shelve all important decisions until later.

14th – Housewives out shopping for the festive season will find many good bargains in their own neighbourhoods. This is one day when tradespeople should be watched, as they are likely to short-change and cheat.

15th – Attend to matters that are in danger of being neglected; this is not a time for putting anything off. Those working around the home should be on their guard against having minor accidents.

16th – Try to spend today resting. You are in dire need of some relaxation, so put off visiting friends and relatives. Partners will be cooperative and will bend to your every whim.

17th – A good day for getting other people to do your bidding. Colleagues will grant favours and take some of the load off your shoulders. Those working from home will be subject to interruption and delay.

18th – Not a favourable day for putting finances at risk – do not become involved in the harebrained schemes of friends or colleagues. Cash is hard to come by and it certainly won't come to you for doing nothing.

19th – Housewives spending time away from home are likely to lose certain personal possessions. Also, the home should be well secured before leaving. This afternoon is a bad time for those dealing with foreigners.

20th – An unexpected cheque or bonus will lift your finances out of the mire. Try to be thrifty, as you are going to need all the cash you can lay your hands on over the festive period and beyond.

21st – Do not allow other people to slow you down – set your own pace and stick to it. You could become unpopular if you refuse to lend others a helping hand, so be tactful.

22nd – Do not waste time or energy on jobs that are proving difficult to complete. Call in a professional to finish them off. Housewives will be out on last-minute shopping jaunts; bargains are hard to come by.

23rd – A quiet day that should be spent planning your festive entertainment. Friends who do drop by will be made welcome. This evening is a good time for getting together with those younger than yourself.

24th – This is New Moon day – a good omen for the festive season for you. However, you may be in a rather reclusive mood; perhaps you are attempting to rest up before the mad whirl begins.

25th – MERRY CHRISTMAS! When you enjoy yourself you really let your hair down, and today will be just like that. Friends will find your antics difficult to believe considering your behaviour over the past few weeks, but you will be enjoying yourself and that's all that counts.

26th – Continue the party-going throughout the day. Friends and partners will be only too eager to join in with you. This afternoon is a good time for getting the family around you.

27th – Not a day when you will feel like doing very much. Attend only to routine jobs around the house, and where possible get out into the fresh air and blow away those cobwebs.

28th – Efforts to overcome family problems will be successful, especially with the aid of a good friend. Do not pay any attention to financial advice given by those younger than yourself.

29th – A good day for attending sporting fixtures. Those who are connected with professional sport in any way will have a successful time. This evening is favourable for getting together with friends and relatives.

30th – Colleagues will be only too willing to lend a hand with arrangements for New Year's Eve parties. Some of you will probably be going to visit others over this period, and arrangements should be made now – leave nothing to chance.

31st – Not the best day of the year financially, but that will not be a major worry at present. Arrangements made for entertainment will work out exactly as planned. Over-indulgence is your only enemy – and this evening! HAPPY NEW YEAR!

The Moon and Your Moods

Our moods are clearly affected by the Moon. After all, why on earth should such a well-balanced person as yourself be, on certain days, bad tempered, nervy, emotional, frigid and sentimental? Well, I'm afraid it is all down to the man in the Moon. Prove it for yourself. Take a look at the Moon table then put it away for a month. In the meantime make notes of your moods, then rescue the table and you will notice a clear pattern of behaviour. You don't need an astrologer to work out for you that, during the month while you were making notes, the Moon was in Scorpio when you were feeling depressed, in Cancer when you were feeling romantic, in Aries when you were bad tempered, et cetera. Your own individual pattern will be repeated each month; but do not be surprised if you are unaffected when the Moon passes through, for example, Aries or Libra. Such a happening would merely indicate that these two signs are not particularly prominent on your birth chart.

Female readers would probably like to take a note of the fact that their menstrual cycle, if normal length, will begin when the Moon is in the same sign each month. Why not have a try? You could find out a lot about yourself.

Moon Tables and Your Moods 1992

Jan	Feb	Mar	Apr	May	June	July	Aug	Sept	Oct	Nov	Dec	
												1
												2
												3
												4
												5
												6
												7
												8
												9
												10
												11
												12
												13
												14
												15
												16
												17
												18
												19
												20
												21
												22
												23
												24
												25
												26
												27
												28
												29
												30
												31

Aries Leo   Sagittarius

Taurus Virgo   Capricorn

 Gemini Libra Aquarius

Cancer Scorpio Pisces

Full and New Moons 1992

January	4th new in	♑
	19th full in	♋
February	3rd new in	♒
	18th full in	♌
March	4th new in	♓
	18th full in	♍
April	3rd new in	♈
	17th full in	♎
May	2nd new in	♉
	16th full in	♏
June	1st new in	♊
	15th full in	♐
	30th new in	♋
July	14th full in	♑
	29th new in	♌
August	13th full in	♒
	28th new in	♍
September	12th full in	♓
	26th new in	♎
October	11th full in	♈
	25th new in	♏
November	10th full in	♉
	24th new in	♐
December	9th full in	♊
	24th new in	♑

Key

♈ Aries	♌ Leo	♐ Sagittarius
♉ Taurus	♍ Virgo	♑ Capricorn
♊ Gemini	♎ Libra	♒ Aquarius
♋ Cancer	♏ Scorpio	♓ Pisces

All Pan books are available at your local bookshop or newsagent, or can be ordered direct from the publisher. Indicate the number of copies required and fill in the form below.

Send to: **CS Department, Pan Books Ltd., P.O. Box 40, Basingstoke, Hants. RG21 2YT.**

or phone: 0256 469551 (Ansaphone), quoting title, author and Credit Card number.

Please enclose a remittance* to the value of the cover price plus: 60p for the first book plus 30p per copy for each additional book ordered to a maximum charge of £2.40 to cover postage and packing.

*Payment may be made in sterling by UK personal cheque, postal order, sterling draft or international money order, made payable to Pan Books Ltd.

Alternatively by Barclaycard/Access:

Card No.

Signature:

Applicable only in the UK and Republic of Ireland.

While every effort is made to keep prices low, it is sometimes necessary to increase prices at short notice. Pan Books reserve the right to show on covers and charge new retail prices which may differ from those advertised in the text or elsewhere.

NAME AND ADDRESS IN BLOCK LETTERS PLEASE:

....

Name ————————————————————————

Address ———————————————————————

————————————————————————————

————————————————————————————

————————————————————————————

3/87